CONTENTS

- Investment in product development and capital equipment
- Debt & finance restructuring
- Keep key stakeholders informed

A sense of urgency
A great day at the Monaco Grand Prix

"Left or right?"
"Awful Management" checklists
Conclusion

Acknowledgements:

Everyone I've ever worked with ... for the fun/challenge
Family and Friends ... for the fun & support
Kino Studios (www.Kino-Studios.com) ... for the fun cartoons
Bluestorm (www.Bluestormdesign.co.uk) ... for the marketing fun
Key Data (www.Keydatasolutions.co.uk) ... for the website fun
Proof Angel (www.the-proof-angel.co.uk) ... for the editing fun

A big "Thank you" to all readers of "Awful Management".

FOREWORD

"Awful Management" is awful.
The vision is "Excellent Management" across the world!

This book is dedicated to the billions of employees currently working within "Awful Management" regimes. The aim is to assist employees, managers, directors, shareholders, unions, and governments – to bring about the death of "Awful Management".

The book also aims to improve the performance of all individuals within an organization, and therefore improve the performance of the organization itself.

"Awful Management" shares my stories, observations and emotions along the journey from a farm worker, in cold rainy fields, right through to a plc Chairman in a warm boardroom. Like some of the awful managers I have met, I didn't always get it right, but thankfully, "you never fail, you learn"!

I hope that this book helps to speed up the attack on "Awful Management", leading to better, harmonious working conditions, and increasing wealth and happiness for all: a truly symbiotic approach. I also hope that the anecdotes prove entertaining and that your investment serves to educate. After all, "life is a growth school".

Enjoy and Good Luck!

Gary

Dr Gary Sheard BSc, PhD, CEng, MIMM

Managing Director - Sheard European Management
Consultants Limited

www.semcltd.com

January 2014

VISION

Chapter 1 - VISION

Early beginnings

It was a cold and rainy September day.

It was my first ever day at work. I was eight years old and standing in the middle of a Yorkshire pea-field. The tops of my badly fitting Wellingtons were rubbing progressively through young white skin, exposing the reddening flesh beneath. The mud weighed heavy around my feet. I slowly dragged myself, and the half-empty sack of peas, around the field. The rain was soaking everything: the field, the peas, my clothes, and the cold wet depressed "me"!

It was summer and school holiday time. Dad was "bloody fed-up" with me under his feet. He therefore decided I should be kicked out of the house, and sent to earn money for the family coffers. In the sixties it was the local summer tradition for us kids to go, into the fields of Yorkshire, "pea-pulling" - or "pea-picking" if you were posh.

To go "pulling" you had to get up bright and early. By 6.00 a.m. you were racing out of the house to the end of the street. There you waited, with one eye open, for the "pea-bus", a tractor pulling an open backed trailer. This ad-hoc transport would then take the workers to the dew-laden fields, where the fat peas hung from their vines, ready for picking. You started the day all lined up at the edge of the field, and then slowly proceeded together across the field, steadily pulling up the vines, picking off the peas, and putting them into your sack as you went along. When your sack was full, you then took it to the "weigh-man", and if it weighed 40 pounds he paid you two shillings - about 10p in new money or 4 Snickers Bars in old money. We called them Marathon Bars then.

Sounds straightforward enough!

However, I was eight. I didn't have a clue about the system. No one had shown me "how to go on". I was wet. I was cold. I was on my own. I had no motivation whatsoever. I didn't even know if a proportion of any two shillings was going to be mine. I just wanted to go home, get warm, get dry, wait for the sun to shine, go out and play football with my mates!

Needless to say, I spent all day on that field and didn't even manage to fill one sack of peas. They paid me one shilling and six pence for pulling my 30 pounds of peas (that's 7.5p in new money and 3 Snickers Bars in old money). Dad was not very impressed with my efforts, and said so. Mam sent me for a bath - I gave her the money!

I clearly hated my first day at work. But looking back at that awful day, it was filled with many "Awful Management" characteristics:

- I had no motivation to be at work.
- I had no induction or training for the job.
- I had poor working conditions.
- Management never bothered with me.
- Management didn't know who I was.

- I was just a number to fill up the bus.
- I had no vision of where this was taking me.

Thankfully, the next day in the pea-fields was a whole lot better. The sun was shining, and two of my Uncles were back from their one-week holiday in Bridlington. My Uncles were teenage brothers, pea-field experienced, fast, and fun!

They immediately took me in hand, putting me to work between them. They also provided me with a plastic bucket. You could pull peas a lot faster utilizing the wide-open mouth of a plastic bucket. The old pea-sacks were floppy; you could lose a lot of time opening their mouths and being un-productive. The pea-sacks also became heavier and heavier as you filled them. It was far easier to lift a bucket each time you moved, and then decant the over-brimming bucket of peas into the sack.

My Uncles were great fun to be around and they had mates with lots of banter. You didn't notice the hard work so much when everyone was joshing, singing, and joking.

I filled two sacks of peas that day, and took home four shillings - that's 20p in new money and 8 Snickers Bars in old money.

Dad was still not impressed and said so. Mam sent me for a bath – I gave her the money and she gave me some back!

***

My second day at work had been much better than the first. The sun had been out all day, so my working conditions had improved. I had received some "on the job training" from my Uncles, and had been supplied with a bucket – "give us the right tools for the job"! Morale was up, due to camaraderie and the "good crack". Productivity was up - due to all of these factors. I would deal with Father later - when I got bigger!

I had many happy summers pulling peas with my Uncles and all of our mates. Through the years, I got faster at pulling peas, I got bigger, and I became stronger. Then I had a vision...

There are hierarchies in most organizations - the pea-field was no exception. We all started as "pullers". Later, if the farmer noticed that you were a fast puller, strong, and showing intelligence he might ask you to work on the prestigious "weigh-in crew". This crew took the weighed sacks of peas from the weighing scales, and stacked them in fifties, in preparation for collection later in the day.

There were many potential fiddles in the pea-pulling process. The "pullers" were paid by weight. Some of the less scrupulous amongst them had noticed that mud, bricks and stones are just as susceptible to gravity as peas are! Sometimes, this "non-vegetable matter" could mysteriously find its way into the pea-sacks, adding to the weight and payment – unbelievable in such civilized society?

One of the roles of the "weigh-in crew" was to decant the peas from the "pullers" sacks, into clean sacks - for both better presentation and a check on the contents. Being in the "weigh-in crew" was seen as a promotion and "cushy" (easy) by the other "pullers". In this higher role, you were paid at a premium guaranteed rate for the day. You were now staff - no longer a piece-worker paid by measured results.

However, the top job on the pea-field was that of "check-weigher".

This was the highest paid job on the field. As the most senior of positions, the "check-weigher" had responsibility for checking the weights, weighing the filled pea-sacks presented personally to you by the weary puller. Then there was quality control, paying out, and hitting volume targets before the lorries arrived at 3.00 p.m. to take the goods to market. You were in charge of the "weigh-in crew" and everyone on the field. This was management!

An awful "check-weigher" (Management) could have an awful influence on morale for everyone on the field. An enlightened "check-weigher" showing appreciation of quality, saying "well done for another sack picked" and encouraging everyone could always get more from the pullers and the team. There were rival farmers in the district and the pullers would always favour working for some "check-weighers" rather than others. The farmer therefore needed to pick his "management team" very carefully. He needed to attract enough pullers onto the bus every morning - and get his peas pulled.

My personal vision at that young age was – to be the "check-weigher" of a happy pea-pulling crew. Looking back it's clear that when an employee's personal vision aligns with the vision of the business then "Awful Management" will be under threat.

Back in the sixties, and in the pea-field of Yorkshire, there tended to be a major lack of Human Resource Departments, Training, and Development Programmes - common traits in some of the poorer enterprises it has been my pleasure to help during the last thirty-five years. So how was I to rise from being a puller, through to the next level of weighing crew, and onwards to the heady heights of "check-weigher"?

The faster and harder working pullers tended to be favoured for the weighing crew. Sometimes "gobby ones" were chosen for the crew (pullers who said "they could do a more senior role", but couldn't).

Everyone on the crew had to be strong enough to throw forty pound sacks up and onto the backs of well-laden lorries – or over the top, if there was a "gobby one" slacking over the other side – oops!

I'd noticed that if the farmer was on the field he tended to stand in the vicinity of the weighing scales, where the pullers had their sacks weighed and were paid. The farmer only made fleeting visits to the field, as he also had cows and harvesting to look after across the parish. He would talk to the "check-weigher" and see how many sacks of peas had been pulled, generally look at the quality of the peas, and see how much cash was left in the "payout bag". You definitely did not want to run out of money on a field of 200 pea-pullers. These were hard working Yorkshire folk - of a very direct and incisive manner. However, the more bags of peas you pulled then the more chance you would be noticed by the farmer, and the greater the probability of promotion.

From this one story it is already clear how "Awful Management" can be devastating to employees at every level within an organization. It can have a strong negative impact on business and organizational results. It is also important how an individual reacts to such management. We have choices. We can put up with it - because we don't know any better. We can go somewhere else - where the management may be better. We can stay and try to make it better.

I decided to stay with it and copy the practices of the fastest pullers. I kept my head down and backside up (that was how you pulled peas) to become the fastest puller, getting noticed as a hard worker, being civil (but not a creep) if the farmer spoke to me, and generally working to the farmers aim - getting the right quality and quantity of peas on the lorry by 3.00 p.m. The farmer had made this objective clear. We all worked to it, and achieved it most days. He then paid us, took us home on his bus (or on the back of an open trailer!), and brought us back again the next day. A fair day's work, for a fair day's pay.

Eventually, after seven long summers in the pea-fields, and at the sweet age of 15, there I stood - master of all I could survey.

I was "check weigher", in charge of the field. I weighed peas and managed the cash, giving words of encouragement to my fellow workers in a dialect filled with song, old bible words, and ones not allowed before the 9.00 p.m. TV watershed. Facilities had also improved. When it rained, we were allowed back to the bus. However, when it stopped, we were encouraged back to our toils – with sweet dialectical encouragement and flying mud balls. We were however dry!

First taste of industry

It was a balmy July 1970 mid-summer's evening. We had just finished playing football in the park. Tired from my emulations, as the local Bobby Moore, I returned home. After a quick wash, I was lying on the living room carpet, listening to "Cream" on the record player. Dad came into the room - so "Cream" went off. He then flopped onto the sofa and slowly melded into its soft green cushions, evening paper in both hands. Dad started to read. I was about to learn, the hard way, that in the absence of a vision, - "all roads lead to anywhere"!

***

I was 16. I had just finished my GCE examinations, as they were called then. I had no job, and absolutely no idea what I wanted to do with my life or career.

However, Dad was clear that it was now time to contribute on a regular basis to the family upkeep. Going back to school was not an option for me. Dad, after a few minutes of reading the racing results, had turned his pages to the "appointments section". My world was about to change, as these cold, heartless words blew over the top of the newspaper…

"There's a job here for thee Lad, in Leeds, its a trainee metallurgical laboratory technician, whatever that is. You'd better apply!"

After several interviews, tests, and the unbelievable news at the "cough and drop medical" that my tonsils had grown back, I was accepted as a Trainee Metallurgical Technician in Leeds. The brave new world of taxable work had been thrust upon me.

Here was a new world. Now you had to work 47 weeks a year - not just 5 in the summer. This was serious stuff! If you were awfully managed all of the time, this was potentially hell. The good news was the company did have a Personnel Department: Human Resources nowadays. Although, I've never come across a department called In-Human Resources. We had good training and development programmes for the Technicians and Apprentices. However, "Awful Management" has many forms. At tender age of 16 I was about to experience one of its classic forms.

My job as Metallurgical Laboratory Technician consisted mainly of serving the "Boffins" – the University qualified metallurgists. They lived behind glass, desks, and well-stained coffee mugs within the bowels of either the company's development or production departments. They were seen as the intellectual elite; sadly many of them acted like it. My job had several elements including cleaning the coffee mugs, making the coffee or tea, and fetching iced buns from the canteen. Slightly more importantly, I fetched samples for inspection or investigation from the foundry, extrusion, and tube drawing areas. I then had to prepare these samples for investigation by the "Boffins".

***

The company had been founded back in the 1800s. The majority of its products were based on brass and copper for the plumbing and heating industries. The products ranged in size from 25-metre heat exchanger tubes for power stations, down to small brass fittings for domestic central heating systems.

Now at this time, the company was developing a new range of 25-metre heat exchanger tubes, based on the new "wonder-metal" - titanium. The new range was targeted at the lucrative worldwide power station market. Not insignificantly during this period, I was playing for the Works football team every Saturday, and getting kicked to death captaining the Apprentice football team on a Sunday. These two remote worlds, "Boffins" and Works football team, were about to meet – and with tremendous benefits!

A typical heat exchanger tube can be 20 metres long and up to 10 centimetres in diameter. They need to be straight! For some months the "Boffins" had been having problems when drawing the tubes down to smaller diameters. The tubes were coming out like bananas and were of no practical use. Titanium was extremely expensive. Whenever a new development batch of titanium tubes needed to be drawn on the tube drawing benches, the "Boffins" would take over en mass, nudging the operator aside to be ignored! Once again under "Awful Management" we had tubes like bananas.

One afternoon I was in the Development warehouse. This was one of the lairs where, on a clear day, "Boffins" could be found. Outside their windows, on a long narrow bogie, lay a new batch of extruded titanium tubes. One of the "Boffins", upon seeing a young and fit Metallurgical Laboratory Technician through the window shouted, "OY! Sheard! Take those tubes down to the tube-drawing-mill for drawing".

Now, upon reflection, and with knowledge of the bollocking I received later, the instruction was intended as a "transport only instruction". I heard it as a "get the job done instruction". Poor clarity of instruction and specification are tremendous areas for "Awful Management" to flourish. We will come back to these evils later. For now, the "Genie was out of the bottle," and I was on my way, down the long yard, with a bogie full of titanium tubes behind me, and not a "Boffin" in sight.

I reached the allotted tube-drawing bench. My arms were now feeling considerably longer. Painfully, I pushed them back into their welcoming sockets. To my delight, the operator on the bench was Dave - a fellow member of the Works football team. Chatter immediately ensued about last week's game. This carried over into a further discussion about the upcoming Saturday match. Eventually we got around to the matter in hand. I said, "I've been sent by the 'Boffins' to get these tubes drawn."

Dave asked, "Shouldn't we wait for the 'Boffins'?" I said that I had been sent, and told to get on with it - and here were the tubes and the specification sheet for the tubes to be drawn down to!

We continued to chat about football. Dave set about getting the draw-bench and tubes ready for "pulling". When tubes are "pulled" they are stretched, whereas when peas are "pulled" they are picked from the pea-vine – such is the Yorkshire dialect! During this continued chit-chat I naively threw in the question, "Dave, the tubes have been coming out like bananas have you any ideas why?"

"Sure I have," said Dave, "but the 'Boffins' never ask me!"

I was gob smacked! What "Awful Management"!

Dave carried on putting the appropriate die into the tube-drawing machine. The die has a hole in the centre. The tube to be pulled has already got one end squeezed, so that it will go through the hole and poke out at the other side of the die. The highly powered dog then comes up along the machine bed, it bites onto the squeezed bit (the "swaged end"), and then pulls the tube through the hole. Everything has to be properly fitted and aligned before you can pull tubes straight!

Non-engineer readers will know that to curl paper you pull it around a corner. If you are making fancy packages, ribbons can be curled by pulling them over the edge of scissors. The same principle is true for titanium tubes. If the die is not exactly at ninety degrees to the direction of pull, then you will create 25-metre bananas. Dave knew this as he walked over to his cupboard. Within this miniature "Aladdin's cave" were various cigarette packets, and papers that he used as shims, to get the dies correctly aligned. I can't remember which brand of shim Dave used - but then came the moment of truth. Dave pressed the button, the equipment hummed and rattled into action, and the first tube came out – as straight as a die!

An hour or so later, I entered the Development Warehouse. I had a bogie full of straight titanium tubes behind me. The "Boffins" shot out from behind their iced buns, mugs of coffee, desks, glass, and offices onto the warehouse floor. To a man they all shouted, "These tubes are all straight, how did you do that?"

At the age of 16 I had already been fortunate to learn first-hand. "I just asked the bloke on the machine, and he knew how to do it!"

During any change or development process, it's a managerial sin not to involve employees who carry out those tasks every day. It is "Awful Management". Exclusion demoralizes the employee, and it wastes a lot of management time. It also misses the chance to make two and two equal five - as knowledge and intelligence become symbiotic. In my story of the tubes, the "Boffins" had failed to share their vision and goals with the operator. Even worse – they had excluded him completely. However, when two footballers with a shared vision and knowledge got involved – "Job done"!

Tastes don't always travel

Excluding the workforce was one of my first major lessons in "Awful Management". However, Churchill said that "When working with foreign cultures, be very careful. If you believe that you understand a foreign culture, you are very dangerous." I can concur with this excellent warning, based on personal experience.

At the turn of the millennium, I was working as Managing Director of a large, Southern German extruded plastic filament manufacturing business. The business had been recently acquired by our USA parent company. The owners of which had also recently acquired several similar businesses in the USA. They had headhunted me to help acquire complimentary European based businesses, turn them around, grow them, and consolidate them (where appropriate) before selling them on as a more profitable group of companies. I was armed with many years of manufacturing and business experience, several manufacturing based turnarounds, and a tortuous use of the German language. I was also programmed to involve everyone and talk to everyone - based on my early positive experiences of employee involvement in tube pulling. This was a big mistake!

In Germany the first birthday of any real significance is the fiftieth.

This is the recognized age of maturity, and when the big party takes place. Therefore, culturally it is very rare to find a German Managing Director appointed before a fiftieth birthday. It is also common practice that a German Managing Director will have come through the ranks, and will have already served time in every Department of the business. Therefore a German workforce expects the Managing Director to be mature in years and fully knowledgeable about the business. In short, he or she is expected to have all the answers, and to give them!

I hope you can already see where this is going?

Within a few weeks of my arrival we had established a programme of regular reviews and meetings to run the business. At the now tender age of 47, I would sit in the "top chair" at these reviews and meetings.

Although I was "under-age" my Doctor title did win a few more status points with the hierarchical German Team. However, I would from time to time ask the Team members, "What do you think?" or, "Do you have any suggestions?" Invariably, I got little or no response. This was very frustrating, and initially I put it down to my spluttering use of the German language. It was not until a few months into the project, when one of the Directors was brave enough to ask me, "Gary, why do you keep asking us what we think?"

The German Team expected me, as Leader, to know what to do. They expected me to instruct them as to what was required. They would not insult me by offering suggestions, or telling me what to do. They would also certainly not make any suggestions "over their own line manager's head". This was a cultural shock to me. It struck hard into one of my fundamental beliefs about good management - that employees should be involved. I did eventually manage to get my direct reports to open up a little bit. Maybe it was OK for them to treat people of a different culture – differently. But they never changed their approach to each other – and why should they if it had always worked for them? The management problem, on this occasion, came from my own good intentions. I wanted to treat the Germans how I would want to be treated – but "Awful Management" never asks, "I wonder how the employees see this issue?"

Developing a vision
"Beanz meanz...!"

Throughout my lifetime, Heinz has always had great products and great marketing; I still eat some of their products every week. I probably always will. Some foods without Heinz ketchup would be like football without a ball.

Back in the 1990s, I had the good fortune to work at Heinz. They not only had some great marketing, and products, they also used some great management phrases: "hearts and minds", "the spirit and the admin." The latter is where the passion and energy, to achieve a vision or objective, works in harmony with the metrics to monitor progress. A characteristic of "Awful Management" is the lack of both "spirit and admin" – passion and measurement.

A good vision for a business should be based on both. In business it is essential that you know where you are making money now, and where you plan to make it in the future. Therefore, a good vision for the business will be both inspirational, in order get emotional buy in from the team, and based on commercial knowledge – for survival and longevity of the business!

Without a vision for the business or the organization "All roads can lead to anywhere!" The vision for a commercial business may lean more towards growth in profits and market share, whereas the vision for a Government body or charity may favour "the extermination of poverty", or some other humanitarian aim. The great dilemma within the NHS is that many of its staff joined the "caring service" because of their caring natures. They did not join to become commercial experts having to balance budgets. Whereas, in the world of Private Equity and Venture Capital most of the staff joined because they love numbers, investment and doing deals. I have many friends in the NHS and in the Investment Industry but if I'm ill I want the Nurses to look after me please! All organizations need a clear achievable vision and the appropriate people to deliver it. In addition, commercial organizations need to ensure their vision is based on good numbers.

It is Government's job to develop visions and policies for the public sector, e.g. "improving people's lives with the money available". We will concentrate on developing a vision for a commercial enterprise.

A commercial enterprise run by "Awful Management" will have few answers to the following questions:

- Where do we make profits now?
- Where could we make more profit in the future?
- What will the future look like when we get there?
- Do we have a vision employees are passionate about?

To take the business out of "darkness and into the light", we need to be able to answer all of these questions...

Developing a vision...*where do we make profits now?*

When you are young, a visit to the pantomime is very exciting. The scenery all looks like the real thing. Some years later, sadly, you realize that it's all a façade. Just like plastic fruit -there is a skin but no apple. Board Meetings at businesses where I've newly arrived as the Turnaround Manager or Chairman have been similar. There can be very good scenery on show – but by the intermission, you have realized that it's "a bit of an act", and some of the actors are "past it".

An investment contact asked me to go and have a look at a manufacturing plant in the North East. They had recently acquired the plant and it was losing money fast. The Managing Director was good enough to invite me along to the next monthly site management meeting. This was my first chance to see the Team "in theatre".

The meeting room was typical of thousands across the country, with a long table down the middle, a plate of biscuits at both ends, and the smell of coffee wafting in the air. There were about eight or nine in the management team and the Managing Director sat at the head of the table. I positioned myself down the "deep end", to ensure a good view of proceedings.

The meeting had an agenda! A good start. We started the meeting on time! Going well. No signs of "Awful Management" thus far! Then the Managing Director asked the person to his left for their report – and off we went, slowly clockwise, around the room. The quality of reporting ranged from verbal only, through to verbal supported with written material. But generally, each Manager was there to remorselessly drone out their problems, apportion blame, and defend themselves when counter-blamed. Morale was low!

This was a classic "effing moaning session".

I listened to the ever-increasing pile of problems and blame. The Managing Director's face became redder and redder with embarrassment. The coffee and biscuit consumption increased, as the nervous tension in the room increased to breaking point. I broke first. I could take it no longer!

"Lady and Gentlemen, why are we all here?" I asked. There was a long silence, so I proceeded to ask each of the Managers, in turn, the same question. The answers were commercially sad - but enlightening.

The Sales Manager said that he was employed to keep those new extrusion machines busy with work. He had been told to do "whatever it takes" to keep business coming in. He had dropped his prices to beat the competition to recent contracts, and the machines were now busy.

The Production manager said the new machines were a good investment and that he was employed to keep those machines running, no matter what! He continued to say the new orders, from the Sales Manager, were for a specification they had never run before. This was causing problems, with increased waste, slower output, and increased overtime. But everyone was extremely busy!

The Finance Manager said that he was there to keep the score. He was very depressed with the results. He was even more depressed because nobody in the Management Team ever asked him how things were going. However, the accounts were all up to date - although they showed a dreadful picture.

Finally it was the Managing Director's turn and he said, "Aren't we all here to make a profit?" I shouted, "HALLELUJAH! Yes, we are all here to help the business make a profit!"

I went on to ask if we had "standard costings" for all of the products.

For the non-accountant, this is simply the cost to make and supply the products. Your selling price for your product should exceed the standard cost – that way you make a profit! Now, in most "Awfully Managed" businesses, the standard cost files tend to be in disarray. It requires constant diligence, and attention by all of the Management Team to keep these files up to date. Raw material prices, outputs, yields and cost of labour change over time. However, fundamental to making profits is that standard costs must be up-to-date!

Incredibly, when questioned, the Finance Manager said, "All of the standard costings are up-to-date." Being slightly suspicious by nature, I decided to invoke a very wise Russian proverb – "Trust but audit," and asked to see the file. Much to my surprise he had the file. All of the data was there, all of the data was up-to-date, but he had never shared the data with any of the Team! He was the accountant and he knew its relevance. You have to educate your people in order to develop them, and so they can develop the business.

Upon investigation, it transpired that only two of the four extrusion lines were making a profit. The other two were making big losses. The more business that they pushed through these two machines - the bigger the losses became. With loss-making products the simple options are to put up the sales price, to reduce costs (through lower purchase prices, yield improvements, or better productivity), a combination of those two, or if you can't make a profit with the product - then stop making and selling it. In turnaround management terms, "Work them up or work them out."

Sadly, after a couple of months wrestling with this problem site, it was agreed that the two profitable extrusion lines would be moved to the main manufacturing site, two of the extrusion lines would be sold to generate cash, and the site would be closed. Redundancies were made, and notice given on a thankfully short lease. I hate to see sites after the people and machines have been moved out. They are like cold and damp graveyards - lifeless with echoes of the past. Everywhere you look - hopes and dreams have gone forever!

I said earlier that one of the characteristics of "Awful Management" is not knowing where the business makes a profit or loss. What was really sad about this case was that the Financial Manager did know, but had not shared with the Team his accurate and timely knowledge of the standard costs, and his thoughts on the mad direction that they were travelling. In addition, the Team were not clear that the top priority was to make a profit. The sharing of this simple vision, and product standard costings, could have greatly improved the performance and longevity of this site.

"Awful Management" eventually fails due a lack of "spirit and admin/"hearts and minds." Employees need a vision, and to be passionately motivated to get there!

Developing a vision...*where could we make more profit in the future?*

Trevor John Francis and myself were born in 1954. He became a great English footballer. At the age of 16 he completely cheesed me off, making his professional football debut, playing for Birmingham City Football Club! Up until this point, nobody younger than me was playing professional football. I therefore still believed, like every other young bloke on our street, that there was still a slim chance of becoming a professional footballer.

However, here was Trevor, only two months older than me, making it to the big time! My mates & I all lived and breathed football, but no matter how much we aspired to be Trevor John Francis, or Bobby

Moore, or Billy Bremner, or George Best, or whoever your local star was, we were not going to make it. Sadly, no matter how many self-help books you read and with phrases like "if you can dream it you can do it," there is still only one Sports Personality of the Year. It's good to dream, and to strive, but "Batman can't really fly!" Regrettably, "Awful Management" may believe that it can – so long as it continues to ignore the facts.

We saw in the previous story that the more they sold, at a loss, the faster they got into trouble. Before looking to increase sales, we have to be sure that our product standard costs are right. Then we can move forward to answer the question, "Where can we make more profit in the future?"

Involving all of the senior management team, I recommend that they investigate all of the following areas, to come up with answers and approaches, agreed by the whole team:

1. Have we "worked up or out" any loss making products?
2. Can we sell more of the profitable products to existing customers?
3. Can we sell more of the profitable products to new customers?
4. Can we sell more of the profitable products to new markets?
5. Can we sell new profitable products to the above?

An "Awful Management" trait can be the absence of regular reviews of these questions. Good management practice is characterized by regular reviews of all product costings and the opportunities to increase product profitability. "Awful Management" lives in the land of "Myth and Legend" driven by sloth.

Developing a vision...*what will the future look like when we get there?*

I love the line from one Christmas song, "It's the most wonderful time of the Year!" Yes - Budget Time!

"Awful Management" hates budget time. It has to spend minutes, hours, and days developing budgets. This requires extended periods of attention to detail. If you're not analytical, it can be as boring as hell. If you are analytical it can be wonderful! However, it is absolutely essential for the good running of the business, and the more accurate and realistic the better.

One of my favourite films is "Apollo 13". There are many business parallels in that story, particularly in the quality and engineering areas. Part of the "Apollo 13" story has parallels to budgeting. I'm thinking about where the Astronauts are trying to work out the jet-thrust timings. They need to get the re-entry angle of the returning space capsule just right. One of the guys in Control Center says, "Too hot and they burn, too light and they bounce right off of the atmosphere, and shoot out into deep space!" Yes, just like annual budgeting! You don't want to be too light and you do not want to be too hot.

Try to get the balance right, but like any forecast it will eventually be wrong. You need to go through the process with the Team. This should always start with the Sales Forecast and then subsequently with each Departmental Manager. "Awful Management" of this process consists of the Managing Director, and possibly the Finance Director, sitting in an office away from the remaining Management Team, without the inputs, commitment, knowledge and experience of the Management Team. The budget produced in isolation is then e-mailed, as an Appendix, to the rest of the Management Team. The covering e-mail says, "Here is the finalized budget - get on with it, or else!"

However, a good Annual Profit and Loss Budget will include the following key elements, ideally produced with the involvement and commitment of the entire Management Team:

1. Sales Forecast - and notes on key drivers
2. Marketing Plan - to support the Sales Forecast
3. Operational/Factory Costs
4. Overhead Costs
5. Finance Costs
6. Capital Investments and Depreciation Plan
7. Other outgoings
8. Retained profit for the business

A Balance Sheet Budget, accompanying the Profit and Loss Budget, will include the following:

1. Debtors   - and notes on key drivers
2. Creditors - and notes on key drivers

3. Stock   - and notes on key drivers

4. Cash Headroom at the end of each month

From the list above, "Cash Headroom" is the most important. Its neglect can lead to "many deaths!" It is a common failing in businesses that Management's awareness of the need to generate a profit has always been greater than its need to generate cash. Yet you can survive for a while without profit, but not cash! "Awful Management" practices will, eventually, result in the running out of cash, and the end of the business. Therefore, budgeting is a vital part of the safety process – to make sure that you always have cash.

The "Annual budget" is a 12-month forecast, a professional best guess. However, for many businesses it is necessary to take a longer-term view. This may be because it takes several years to develop a new product, expand a new market, re-equip a property, or develop a new site. It is for this reason that "5-Year-Plans" become necessary. They are also essential where additional funding is required for the plan. In the absence of a plan, Banks, Venture Capitalists, and Private Equity Houses will not look at investing.

When business profits and cash are limited, the business may well need additional funding to support capital investment and the long-term future. Having available a good quality "5-Year-Plan" is an essential tool in the management's toolbox. It is negligent otherwise.

Without investment in the future, there will be no future.

I still have an old slide-rule - but they don't make them any more. "Awful Management" does not invest in the future.

Developing a vision...*do we have a vision employees are passionate about?*

There is a big difference between "French-kissing" the girlfriend and shaking hands with a visiting product supplier. Imagine getting these two the wrong way around – awful!

Many years ago, back in one of the World's many conflicts, there were two army sergeants. The sergeants stood, each with their own troops, at either end of the same long muddy trench. One sergeant is telling his soldiers, "When you go over the top it's very muddy, cold and wet up there. The enemy will be firing very accurately. Their bullets are deadly, and come at you twenty per second. The likelihood of coming back alive, or unharmed, is very remote. You will probably die!"

At the other end of the trench, a lively and enthusiastic sergeant is telling his soldiers, "Here is your big chance to show what you can do. The enemy has been killing your mates. They have been taking your wives for pleasure. They have been letting your children go cold, hungry and starve. Here is your big chance to put it all right, to take revenge on these cold heartless devils, and to rip their guts out."

"Let's go take that hill!"

It's clear which of the two groups will have the passion to succeed.

The second group not only had a clear vision, "taking that hill". They also had the passion and motivation to achieve it. The troops under the negative sergeant, with the "Awful Management" approach, were already dead in their minds before they even set-off. A clear vision, "bought into" by a passionate and enthusiastic team, brings success.

There are hundreds of books about "Vision Statements" and "Mission Statements". It is not my intention to duplicate their excellent work. We all know how to search on Amazon for books! My major point is, "Awful Management" has no vision for the business, no route plan to get there, no 5-Year-Plan to support their journey, and definitely no passionate team, "bought in" to achieve any of it.

***

A good vision statement should be aspirational in nature, clear in its primary goal for the organization, and be an inspiration for the daily operations and thinking of all employees.

If you type "example vision statements" into any search engine, there are many good examples of aspirational vision statements that inspire, enthuse, and unify all employees behind one common goal.

I list a few of my favourite vision statements below:

- A personal computer in every home, running Microsoft software
- To help people be healthy
- To have our product in every home
- To make people happy
- Equality for everyone
- Improving people's lives

One of my personal favourites comes from Shakespeare's Henry the Fifth. The young King Henry, new to the throne, is looking for an inspirational vision which both he and his Barons can rally behind. Henry comes up with a very simple vision, "To defeat the French!"

It is simple, it promotes passion, and it is backed up with bonuses - new lands and plunder for the Barons. Today it is probably politically incorrect. Such a vision statement, if Shakespeare were still alive, would now read, "Death to all Klingons!"

Chapter 1 – "Awful Management" Checklist

1. Be unclear which products make money.
2. Have no clear vision for the business.
3. Avoid budgeting and 5-Year-Plans.
4. Do not share any hopes or dreams with the Team.
5. Particularly, do not engage or enthuse any Team Members.

ORGANIZATION

Chapter 2 - ORGANIZATION

Baptism by fire

"I want you to fire that useless b*****d!" bellowed my new boss.

It was early on my first day as Assistant Quality Manager. I'd already had the obligatory cup of tea - followed by the short "rally to the flag" speech. Now I was being shown around this very old, large, dark, Dickensian factory.

My new employer was part of a massive plc group. Our division made large, complex, pieces of electrical equipment – destined for power stations around the World. This was the early 1980s and the unions were at the peak of their power. We were based in Manchester - a power centre for the unions at the time.

I had decided to move from previous "Techie" roles, into the wider world of industrial relations and man-management. I had now been appointed Assistant Quality Manager, reporting to the Quality Manager. One of my major responsibilities was the management of 40 mechanical inspectors and 35 electrical testers. The Quality Manager reported to the Managing Director – the one bellowing that "I want you to fire useless b*****d."

It transpired that the Managing Director hated the unions. The gentleman at the focus of his early morning hatred was the Shop Steward for the Electrical Testers. The Managing Director was only one stride away from the Shop Steward, looking straight into his eyes as he unleashed his nasty tongue. I remember that, such was the tension between these two, the Shop Steward just turned away and half-whispered, "No, you're the b*****d."

I remember thinking none of this stuff had come up during the interview process. However, I had just seen, and just one foot in front of my face, what real top notch "Awful Management" looked like. They say that you tend to adopt the approach of your role models. Somehow, this didn't look or feel right. It wasn't right. I will come on to working positively with the unions in the next chapter. But for now back to the world of "Savage Amusement," a phrase often used by Ken - my very first mentor.

Having completed the tour of the factory, the two of us returned to the Managing Director's office. A second cup of tea arrived – no biscuits at this level. By now I was wondering where my new boss was – the Quality Manager. It transpired he was on holiday for the next week.

The Managing Director saw this absence as his chance - to steer the future of the Quality Department.

It appeared that the Managing Director was not pleased with the current Quality Manager's performance. He wanted me to take over the Quality Manager's job – and soon! I was in my late twenties. The opportunity for a rapid promotion sounded very exciting. However, when I look back, this was further

"Awful Management" in action. The Managing Director had never discussed performance with the Quality Manager. He had never given him an official warning. He had never offered management training, or development, to the Quality Manager. He had definitely not told the Quality Manager, straight to his face - he could lose his job if he didn't pull his socks up.

A week later, the Quality Manager returned from his holiday. He was a nice enough guy, a very good engineer, but man management was not his forte. We developed a reasonable working relationship. He focused on the quality engineering issues, and I concentrated on the management and quality systems issues. However, there was always a slight under-current of tension in our discussions. The Quality Manager was twenty years older than me. He realized that the "young buck" may have been brought in to take over his job. I knew this to be the case, but had been told, threateningly, to keep my mouth shut – an "Awful Management" nasty habit.

At its peak, the site had employed over 17,000. It was straight from a Lowry painting. Large old buildings, big iron factory gates, and high brown brick offices that included a restaurant, with 6 status levels, for lunchtime dining - truly "Awful Management". Our division included tall aircraft-hanger like factory buildings. The half brick, half-corrugated buildings shrouded the welding shop, machine shop, assembly shop and electrical-mechanical testing area. Within the factory buildings, electric overhead cranes buzzed and hummed as they rolled above the workforce. These giants in the ceiling, slowly and elegantly, transported large pieces of equipment up, over, and across the shop floor.

It was an exciting and fabulous place. Actors love, "the smell of the grease-paint". I love the smell of burning welding electrodes, soluble-oil, and the heady mix of factory fumes and solvents. In addition, always in the background the constant banging of hammers, the zip of electric-arc electrodes firing up, lathes stopping and starting, spanners being dropped, and the hum of progress as the cranes moved the various parts to the assembly department and final conclusion - shipping. There were, of course, headier attacks on the senses. Sulphur smells from aged oils breaking down, the eye watering sting of vaporized urine in the cold, dark, dank toilets, and stained teacups, grimy from years of tannin attack and lack of cleaning. This was a real engineering factory!

The Quality Department consisted of three elements: mechanical inspectors, electrical testers, and a small group of quality engineers. The Quality Manager managed the quality engineers. I managed the 75 strong groups of inspectors and testers - all highly unionized!

For the first few months, it was all about "finding your feet", meeting people, and understanding how the processes worked. The time flew by quickly, and it was all new and interesting. The technology was also very exciting. We could create our own lightening! In the Electrical Test Department, we had to generate very high voltages. The test equipment created electric arcs that would go zinging and crackling 4 to 5 metres through the air. However, in the back of my mind was the Managing Director's comment that at some point he would want me to take over as the Quality Manager. Therefore, I had two recurring questions in my head. When? How will we know when we get there?

Managing - but what?

This got me to thinking and, after a few weeks of frustration, I decided the best way forward would be to show them I'm doing a good job! The first problem was nobody had actually told me what my job was. They had told me my job title. However, I had nothing telling me my responsibilities and aims/objectives. This is classic "Awful Management" – just give them a job title and expect miracles.

The only objective I had been given so far was "sack the gentleman allegedly born out of wedlock." This was just pure bravado and stupidity. Also since that first uncomfortable morning, the Managing Director had not mentioned it again.

It didn't seem right to sack anyone without real cause, evidence, and the following of a proper HR process. I decided that the sacking of the Shop Steward was neither the right thing to do, nor the route to the top. In deep thought, I wandered down to the tea-machine, got a cup of "hot and wet," and pondered again - what was my job?

I had no job description, so I decided to figure it out for myself.

I was the Assistant Quality Manager. There might be clues in the title. Yes. Quality and Management. On the quality front, it was important that we had no customer returns, no complaints, no scrap and no rework. But Boy! We were not in that arena. We had lots of opportunities. Clearly it was important to attack (show spirit as Heinz would say) all of these areas, and to show improvement (admin). On the management front, I was in charge of 75 employees, their costs, their motivation and discipline.

Some people think verbally. Some people think visually. I love graphs! I decided to start plotting graphs for each of the above key areas, on a monthly basis. I figured that in the absence of clear targets, I could at least show the trend of any improvements we made. I also figured it's not just the graphs themselves that are important, it's what I was going to do to improve them. Graphs are motivational. If they are going the right way, they motivate you. If they are going the wrong way, they really motivate you.

Within a few months, the graphs were starting to make sense. I decided to collate them all, within a fancy new black plastic binder. These were new on the market in the early eighties. Inside the binder were 20 clear plastic display pockets - ideal for holding and presenting my data and graphs. In the early 1980s, personal computers (PCs) were still quite rare. All of the graphs had to be drawn by hand, coloured in (using newly available fluorescent pens), and collated. I was very proud of what came to be called the "Black Book".

Inside the front cover of the "Black Book" was the contents page. The page listed labour costs against budget, customer complaints, rework costs, scrap costs, and new ideas. In its simplest form, I had developed my own job description. The inferred goal was to improve from where we were today. The goals had not yet been defined numerically. However, better than yesterday - is better!

On subsequent pairs of facing pages on the right hand page was a graph, and on the left hand page were the actions underway to improve the graphic results. At a glance you could see performance against budget, the trend, and "what the hell you were doing about it!" I now had in one book my job description, objectives, and I could show how I was making progress. Fantastic, but "Awful Management" was about to intervene in a ruthless fashion.

Change can be good news

Somehow, our "highly charged" Managing Director got kicked upstairs. There was an organizational shuffle. My boss (the Quality Manager) would now report to the new Manufacturing Director. There were several days of middle management meetings. The newly appointed Director wrestled with his inherited team, a strongly unionized environment, and an old-fashioned engineering business. I had watched this game from the stands – a little scared.

Eventually my boss was summoned to his first meeting with the new Manufacturing Director. Then, one of the worst moments of my working career played out in front of my eyes like a bad dream!

"I want your Black Book!" demanded the Quality Manager. "Why?" I asked. "To show the new Director what we do in this department, and the progress we are making!" My heart sank! This cold hearted, calculating child of allegedly unmarried parents, was attempting to nick all of my work, take all of the praise, and all of the adulation. "B*****d!" This was really "Awful Management".

For the rest of that day, I just couldn't think straight. I couldn't concentrate. I was angry. I was sad. Driving home that evening I was determined to go and look for a new job. That is what "Awful Management" does to people. It gets them upset, it demoralizes them, they become unproductive, and they leave – a shame and a waste. I didn't sleep well that night but "tomorrow would be another day".

I got into work early the next morning. I asked the Quality Manager for my "Black Book" back, and also how he had got on with the new Manufacturing Director? It transpired that my boss had never got to see the Manufacturing Director, who had been called away to a Senior Meeting. So my boss never got to steal my work, and due to his imminent holidays, and as you will see, I got there first – "Praise the Lord!"

Back in the early eighties it was still common practice to have typing pools, or to share the services of a secretary. The Factory Managers and the Manufacturing Director all shared the same secretary. She sat and worked just outside the Manufacturing Director's office.

My boss was still on holiday. This particular morning the birds were singing loudly and the sun was shining brightly. Although it was probably raining – it was Manchester after all. But I include this late-spring imagery for dramatic effect. I needed to collect some typing. Up until this point, I had not met the new Manufacturing Director. However, as I walked in to the secretary's office – there he was. "Good morning, I'm the new Manufacturing Director, who are you?" he asked. Surprised I said, "Oh! Hello. I'm Gary Sheard, the Assistant Quality Manager." Smiling at me he continued, "Would you like to come into my office, and tell me what you do?" "Sure," I replied excitedly.

I had my "Black Book" tightly tucked under my arm. I sat down, tea and biscuits arrived, and I opened the book. Slowly, as I showed him the graphs, and the planned actions, a wry smile formed across his face. This was his style of management too!

The very next month, I was sent on a two-week "Management Development Course" to the wilds of Dunchurch. The story of those two, truly action packed, weeks could be the source of a good book - but potentially too "writ-tempting." Suffice to say, the fortnight included threatening a HR Manager with defenestration (death from being thrown through a high window), a Sales Director breaking his arm, and a Lord of the realm being very upset when mistaken for a Sales Manager (by me)! However, when I returned from the course the Quality Manager had been transferred to the Quality Assurance Department. He was to spend his time out at foreign suppliers, looking at the quality of aluminium castings. I was promoted to Quality Manager – hooray! But there was catch?

At this time we were making high voltage switchgear. This was big and exciting equipment. It was also potentially lethal. When you think that 240 Volts can kill you (standard UK domestic voltage), just think what 750,000 Volts would do to you! This was the kind of equipment we were making. Safety, quality and reliability were paramount, and on the top of everyone's work agenda.

Partly because I was young, and partly because there was a growing belief that quality personnel should not report to manufacturing personnel (foxes in charge of the hen house), I was made Quality Manager. This was on the understanding that I would report to the Manufacturing Director for my daily line duties, and to the Quality Assurance Manager for clarity on quality matters. Sod it, now I had got two bosses!

The "Good Book" says, "No man can be the servant of two masters: for he will have hate for the one and love for the other; or else he will hold to the one, and despise the other."

Both the Manufacturing Director and the Quality Assurance Manager were great guys. They were both very good at what they did. I was fortunate to learn a lot from both of them. However, human beings are human beings, and we don't all have the same priorities. I became the "Stretcher Armstrong" of quality - being pulled this way and that, by my two bosses. When one wanted an urgent shipment making, the other wanted time to "make sure." Both were right, but I couldn't be in two places at once. With two bosses, the job was proving impossible. "Awful Management" had got me reporting to two bosses!

"Meetings bloody meetings"

It's awful to be unclear what your job is. It's awful to be unclear what your goals and targets are. But even more awful was the Wednesday morning Management Meeting. The meeting was chaired by our never static, highly charged, Managing Director - let's call him M.

For the masochists, 10.00 a.m. every Wednesday morning must have been the highlight of the week. For the rest of us - shear hell. We would all gradually assemble between 9.59 a.m. (guess who?) and 10.15 a.m. (the "Awful Management" crowd). The tension would rise as the "nervously tormented" slowly increased in number. The air would thicken with the smoke from heavily drawn cigarettes, as we prepared for the "Darth Vader like" entrance of M. We will return to this terrifying scene shortly…

In contrast, I remember being taught, rather harshly, the importance of punctuality. This was with a previous employer, where meetings always started on time. I had just joined the company, and in my first management role, as the Quality Manager. This was my first attendance as a Manager at the monthly Management Meeting.

The meeting was planned for the ever popular 10.00 a.m. start. Being untrained, at the time, in the art of punctuality, I started to ready myself just after 10.00 a.m. by pulling my files, reports, bits, and pieces together. This was followed by the obligatory visit to the toilet. These were modern toilets, in a new building. The smell was "murder by lavender and bleach". I was all set for my grand entrance into the meeting room - a roll on the drums please!

The managers were all sitting there, around the board-table, as expected. The Managing Director sat at the head of the table. I shut the door behind me and sat down. There was a tension in the air. The others had been here before. Looking over his glasses, the Managing Director addressed me, "What makes you think you are so important to keep your colleagues waiting?" The guillotine blade had fallen - right on my lily-white neck! I just simply died and wanted the floor to swallow me up. But I never turned up late to his meetings again!

However, back at the meeting for the psychologically disturbed, it was now 10.15 a.m. The office door opened, and M swept in, gliding through the fog of cigarette smoke, to the head of the table. We all sat down. No teas or coffees were ever offered – you had to bring your own. There was no, "Good Morning," there was no, "How are you all?" The meeting always started with the nightmare question – "Where are we up to?"

This was "Awful Management" in theatre and at its best. There was no agenda, we had no clear objectives to report against, there was no data presented. M would simply pick on the first person to flinch, shuffle, or crack. Blame, accusation, counter-accusation, lack of facts, myth, legend, swearing, negative-emotion, were the common currency of the meeting – it was hell!

I remember vividly, at one of these meetings, the IT Manager getting a particularly tough ride. I was sitting opposite the victim, during his battering and abuse by M. To my right, and a couple of chairs down from M sat the Welding Shop Manager - a tremendous Scouser, endowed with legendary humour and mischievousness. During the tirade on our colleague opposite, the Welding Shop Manager surreptitiously wrote something on his notepad. He then pushed it quietly and secretly in front of me. On it he had written, "Smile now and you are dead." I smiled and I was!

This serendipitous flagellation continued for about two hours. M got worse, telling the IT Manager to lie on the table so we could all knock some sense into him! This directive was followed by M almost giving the first ever appraisal, when he screamed, "If I could find all of your replacements on the streets of Manchester today – I'd sack the lot of you!" It was really that bad: truly "Awful Management".

You might quite rightly ask, "But did these bullying methods actually work?" The answer is no. A combination of poor investment in technology (too little too late), and "Awful Management" eventually closed the business. This was a real shame. The parent company had money to invest, and we had great people, but the people had neither the shared vision nor the motivation to get there.

A mantra for management

After three years, in this "highly charged" environment, I felt it was time to move on. We were coming to the end of major contracts and making redundancies. The order book for this old technology was rapidly declining. It was time to polish up the CV. I'd had three very busy, interesting, and intense years with the company. I'd learned a lot, particularly on the man-management side. I wanted to encapsulate it all into a phrase I would never forget. I also wanted to make sure I didn't become an exponent of "Awful Management"!

After lots of attempts, I finally developed the following phrase, which is now my "organizational mantra":

"*Acknowledgement from your boss for a job well done is a great motivator.*"©

When I ask employees, "Do you agree with this?" I get a very high "nod-rate". It's a mantra that's helped thousands of employees, and also earned me a living for the last 30 years. It's a mantra that flies in the face of "Awful Management". It is constructed using four key elements: boss, job, well done, and acknowledgement. Let's look at each of these elements in turn...

*"Acknowledgement from your **boss** for a job well done is a great motivator."*

Remembering that, "You can only serve one master!" You need to start by having a clearly defined organizational structure. It should define who works for whom. Ideally, each person has just one boss. You have really got this right when you can ask any individual in the organization, "Who is your boss?" and they respond with one clear name. I always feel sorry for people working in complex organizations - particularly those working within matrix management. "You can only serve one master!" A nice crisp organizational-chart is the icing on the cake for this one. However, in an "Awful Management" regime – they tend to be "virtual," or "just being put together".

*"Acknowledgement from your boss, for a **job** well done, is a great motivator."*

The second key word is job. I remember the days of the "eight-page job description". Hundreds of them used to be neatly filed in those three high bottle-green filing cabinets. Nobody ever read them, or used them. They were a waste of time and effort - much better to have three or four very simple objectives that clearly define what the employee has to achieve.

Organizations are like oil tankers. They can take a long time to change direction. They often carry on, just as ever before, and don't review or change direction until they approach or hit a problem. If allowed, people will turn up to work tomorrow and just do the same as they did yesterday - and do it without question. They can be on automatic pilot, all day - until home time!

One technique you can apply when starting with a new Management Team is to check that someone manages each of the basics. These basics consist of the Profit and Loss account, Balance Sheet, Cash Flow Forecast, Health and Safety, Quality, and Product Development. It can be quite revealing, when sitting with a new Management Team, to start at the top of the Profit and Loss account and ask the question, "Who is responsible for sales?" and see what answers you get.

Quite often, there are gaps and misunderstandings about who is responsible for what. There can even be key elements of the business that no one is managing - "I thought that someone else was looking after that." When you finally have clarity on who owns the Sales line, then you move on to the next line of the Profit and Loss account. "Who owns purchasing?" and so on down the page. This is great fun, and often a catalyst for real change.

With responsibilities agreed and allocated for all the elements of the Profit and Loss account, you can then move on to review the Balance Sheet, and in the same way. It is frighteningly common to find unallocated areas of responsibility for Balance Sheet items.

Debtors are a classic area for neglect. "I thought it was your responsibility," barks the Sales Manager at the Finance Manager. "No way, it's definitely your responsibility!" shouts back the Finance Manager. "Awful Management" in action.

By carrying out what may sound like a pretty boring process, you will gain clarity for who is responsible for what in the organization. This becomes the beginning of job descriptions/objectives, based on the fundamentals of running the business. I also guarantee that the meeting will be far from boring. Take the first-aid kit with you!

*"Acknowledgement from your boss for a job **well done** is a great motivator."*

Well done is beating budget. Well done is achieving your daily output target. Well done is picking up the phone before it rings four times. Well done is developing a new product, on time and within budgeted cost. Well done can always be defined by a number, such as a budget target, an output target, or in the case of projects, a date. By having clarity of what job means, for each person, and adopting a numerical target to define success for that job, we have good numerical objectives. This is at the heart of good management. It is a pain in the heart for "Awful management".

*"**Acknowledgement** from your boss for a job well done is a great motivator."*

By this stage, you know who your boss is, you know what your key objectives are, and you know your numerical targets for success. However, to be acknowledged by your boss for a job well done, you need to meet with him or her. "Awful Management" are like wasps – they only turn up to annoy, create a scary noise, and sting.

To have a good conversation with your boss you actually need to meet, sit down, and go through where you have been, where you are now, and where you plan to go next – based on facts and figures.

In this incredible age of the "tinternet" it is possible to meet by Skype or Facetime etc. For me, that is not the same as meeting. In this busy world there is seldom enough quality time to actually meet the boss, face to face. The following phrases strike despondency into the hearts of subordinates in need of leadership, "I'm just going to a meeting," or "Sorry, I have to leave now - meeting a client," or "I'm leaving to catch a train".

To be acknowledged, you have to plan to meet on a regular basis with your boss. It may again sound boring and dull, but insist on getting your "one to one" in the diary for the next twelve months. Directors should meet their Chair once a month at the Board Meeting. Managers should meet their Directors once a week and Managers need to see their direct reports on a daily basis. All of this needs diarising. The probability of having a meeting with the boss rises dramatically if it is in the diary.

Why bother with all of this organizational management and diary stuff?

My argument runs thus. In most organizations and businesses, one of the largest costs is people. People determine the direction and the decisions of the organization or business, which again ultimately leverages the success or failure of the enterprise. It is therefore important that the organization is "efficient". How many organizations have 100% clarity of organization? How many organizations have clear job objectives? How many organizations have numerate objectives directly relating to the Profit and Loss account and Balance Sheet? How many bosses religiously review their direct reports for progress against these numerate objectives on a regular diarized basis? If you answered 50% for each of these four questions and do the mathematics, you would quickly come to the conclusion that "Awful

Management" leads to a tremendous loss of employee efficiency.

One day back in the eighties, I was working up in Scotland. I intended to introduce this process to the owner of a manufacturing and service business. I'd spent the last eight hours reviewing the factory, administration, and accounts. At the end of a long day, we sat down together for feedback.

The owner had a tremendous presence. He was a successful businessman, well over six foot tall, and had a beautiful strong accent. This was the first time we'd met. As he lowered himself into a large leather chair, beside the coffee table, he said in a deep challenging tone, "Right son, what do you think you can do for me?"

I carefully, but quickly, took him through my observations and recommendations. This culminated in recommending the need for a clear organization, clear numerate objectives, and regular Monday reviews with each of his direct reports. I also suggested that they should meet as a group, after the individual reviews.

My potential client stood up to his full height. He towered threateningly above me, as I sipped nervously from my elegant coffee cup. Then he took a deep breath and bellowed, "Son, I'm already doing a seventy hour week. Now you want me to do another eight hours with my Team every Monday!"

Challenged but un-phased I replied, "If you spend Mondays reviewing progress with each of your Directors and Senior Managers, followed by a Team Meeting, – they are directed and motivated. What are you going to do with the rest of your week?" He laughed out loud. Soon after, he implemented the mantra. A couple of years later he sold the business to a Top 100 plc.

Developing people

I hate "Awful Management" when it treats employees like dirt, crushes all drive and ambition, and is unfair...

During the early nineties, I became Managing Director of a large garment manufacturing and processing business, part of a major plc. My division employed 2,000 people across several sites. The first day was spent meeting and greeting the senior team at the major site, deep in the heart of Yorkshire. This was a very large site, employing 1,200 people. The large old buildings were red brick, but their colour had changed to dark brown and black – the result of pollution from earlier in the century. Subconsciously, the musical strains of, "And did those feet in ancient times," could be heard. The site was very worn, smoke darkened, and grim – with a capital "G".

It was early morning on my second day. The Factory Manager was due to take me around "His" factory. I'd already heard a few myths about this gentleman, so I was on my guard. I went down to the shop floor to meet him as planned. There stood "erectus arrogantus," with his entourage of lackeys and sycophants surrounding him. After a few mandatory pleasantries, we set off around the untidy, dirty shop floor.

One of my methods for assessing how much management respects the workforce is to ask for a visit to the shop floor toilets. This request met with a lot of resistance, attempted diversions, and stifled giggles. When we finally reached the toilets and became "exposed to the radiation", the reasons for management's earlier feet dragging became clear. A sensory "cac-ophony" and overload for the eyes and nose. However, my golden rule is, "If you wouldn't use the facilities, why should we expect staff to?" I stated that urgent work was needed, and I looked forward to coming back soon, and using the upgraded facilities.

By now, the Factory Manager was becoming uneasy. My gentle questioning of why things were not clean, neat, tidy, good on the eyes, and good on the nose within a garment manufacturing and cleaning business was getting to him. His timid, subservient, entourage appeared frightened stiff to answer any direct questions. Slowly their heads and necks were disappearing into their new white overalls. Not one of them offered an answer, or comment, all morning. However, the Factory Manager then proudly announced that, "We shall now be entering the heart of the operation, the Factory Management Office".

We had spent the last hour looking at badly maintained buildings, decrepit machinery, chaos, and a dirty shop floor. We had seen toilet facilities unfit for animals. What we had seen was "Awful". However, with a roll of the drums, and a fanfare of trumpets, here was the "Factory Management Office". Outside the office door, on the floor, were two mats for wiping your feet. A large sign on the factory side of the office door read:

"Wipe your feet before entering!"

We wiped our feet, the door was opened, and we passed through into another world...

Behind the door was a reception room. On the reception room floor lay a high quality, thick pile, shaggy carpet - spotlessly clean. In the centre of this large palatial room was a glistening glass coffee table, supported by gleaming chrome legs. A beautiful flower arrangement stood on the centre of the coffee table. Three, highly polished, black leather settees surrounded the table. Everywhere in the room shone.

We then went through to the Factory Manager's office, with its en-suite toilet and shower room. The Factory Manager sat behind his large mahogany desk, on his big shiny black leather chair. We all sat down around his boardroom table, each of us sinking into our very comfortable and welcoming leather chairs. His handpicked receptionist came in to the room. She served us politely with coffee. The cups were beautiful white china. The biscuits were top quality. The chocolate was thick. A lapsed chocoholic remembers these things.

We talked for some time about daily targets and what everyone's duties were. All answers were straight from the "Awful Management Handbook". Not one of the Team had ever been trained for their current role. It was clear that the dictatorial Factory Manager wanted to keep it that way. He needed to keep them suppressed and ignorant of a better way. That way he retained his sham of a power base.

Finally, as "the event" drew to a close, I walked back through reception, facing the closed door to the factory. I was about to open the door, but the Factory Manager shouted sarcastically, in showboating fashion, across the heads of his lap dogs, "Doctor, were you impressed with what you've seen?" I thought for a moment, and then replied with full sincerity and passion, "No, the wipe your feet sign is on the wrong side of the door!"

First thing the next morning, the Factory Manager came riding in to town, dismounted his horse outside the sheriff's office, and burst through the half doors to see me.

"Previous Managing Directors have tried to change things here without my support. They all failed. Based on yesterday you and me are not going to get on!" he screamed at the top of his voice.

Having already rehearsed my answer, at least a dozen times that morning, I replied, "You are absolutely right. We are not going to get on. Your job is being absorbed into the Operations Directors role. You are redundant with immediate effect."

Sometimes to change the culture of a team you have to give it new leadership.

During the months that followed, we started to rid the business of its previous "Awful Management" practices. We set about tidying up the organizational structure, setting numerate objectives, holding weekly report meetings and monthly management meeting for the Directors and Senior Management. We also started the brave new world of "Appraisals and Personal Development".

With regular performance monitoring and reviews in place, the opportunity to hold meaningful annual appraisals grows month by month. Both the employee and the manager can see, week-by-week, if progress is being made, where the weaknesses are, and where training and development is needed. With these ongoing reviews (mini-appraisals) in place then the annual appraisal is no longer a place for surprises. It becomes a productive and positive hour or so, to formalize and record progress made, agree numerate objectives for the next 12-months, and list training and development needed in order to supply the employee with skills for the job.

"Awful Management" of annual appraisals goes broadly like this.

The Manager is very busy and has neither the time nor the inclination to carry out an appraisal. However, well after the due date, the company politics eventually coerce the "Awful Manager" to carry out an appraisal. The "Awful Manager" has not been taught the value of carrying out a good appraisal, in terms of benefits for both the appraisee and appraisor. The "Awful Manager" has not been taught how to carry out an appraisal. The lack of good documentation also adds to the awfulness of the process.

So an awful appraisal could be very short and sweet...

Manager	"I don't think you are very good."
Employee	"I think I am"
Manager	"Well trust me - you're not!"

One of the great joys of management, particularly as you get older, is to see the younger people developing and coming through the ranks. The appraisal is a fundamental part of people development. It allows you to take stock of what skills and training the employee needs - to develop their own skills and to develop the organization.

With the Factory Manager removed, we found several of his Team capable of much more. After suitable training and development, they gave more. We also found several suppressed graduates, outside the "Dictatorial Love-In". These were real "golden seeds" for the future. Sometimes there are such employees who, through no fault of their own, have been buried within the organization. They have great potential when directed, managed, trained and developed. It took us about a year to get the place on track. With

"Awful Management" removed, the seedlings began to grow. Even better – we put the sign on the other side of the door!

There are, of course, some people who just don't make it. I firmly believe that you should not write anyone off until they have been given every chance to perform. This involves agreeing objectives with them, reviewing progress on a regular basis, giving training and development where needed, and seeing if the training aids improvement. Only then, if there has been no improvement, it is fair to say, "Look, we have a problem!"

The legal processes for performance managing a person out of an organization are well documented. This is the end of an "Awful Management" road. It was Management that hired the person in the first place, and it's Management's responsibility to give leadership, and support throughout the career of an employee. The more watering, feeding and sunshine you give the plants – the stronger they grow.

Chapter 2 - "Awful Management" Checklist

1. Always be abusive to your employees.
2. Hold meetings without any agenda.
3. Ensure that the organization is unclear.
4. Do not allocate numerate objectives or responsibilities.
5 Never hold performance review meetings.
6. Do not develop or train the employees.
7 Ensure you have the best office. (You have earned it!)
8. Have no concern for employee working conditions.
9 Let the staff think you will run an appraisal process. (But don't.)

UNIONS

Chapter 3 - UNIONS

"Indescribable!"

Both of my Granddads started their working lives in the 1920s. They were both colliers and, as we say in Yorkshire, "They worked darnt pit." When talking about the working conditions down the pit, Granddad Sheard used to rear himself up to his full five foot four inches, screw up his face - in well practiced and remembered pain, and snarl the word, "indescribable!" Granddad would then continue, describing the "indescribable" conditions as follows...

Imagine working in a seam of coal and you are lying on your side. You have a coal pick in your hands, and you are trying to hew out the coal from just in front of your face. There is only a small space between your top shoulder and the free hanging ceiling. Above that ceiling can be over a mile of the planet earth, bearing down with all of its weight and majesty. There is just enough space to allow your arm to rotate backwards and swing the coal pick. You are working mostly alone. There is only the light of your pit lamp to squint by.

There is water everywhere. The water you are lying in is cold and dirty. If you want to go to the toilet, well, the good news is you are already there. Now imagine working like this for five minutes. Then imagine working like this for a full hour. Could you imagine spending eight hours of your life working like that? Well, for my Granddads, and most colliers, that was their working lives. No wonder they liked a pint after work!

Granddad Sheard used to tell us his nightmare story...

One day he was down the pit, on his side, and hewing away at the coal. Suddenly, a large lump of stone fell out of the ceiling directly above him. It fell on top of one hip, crushing him, and trapping him. The pain was unbearable. He was alone and afraid. There was the fear of a further fall that might finish him off. He lay there screaming and shouting for help. After what seemed forever, and just before he passed out, his mates found him. He was one of the lucky ones. They dug him out, they got him back up to the surface, and they got him home. There was no NHS, so Granddad was left, writhing and screaming, on his bed at home – comforted by my ever-resourceful Gran.

After a week at home, there was little improvement in Granddad's condition. Gran decided to take matters into her own hands. Specialists cost money. Colliers were poor people, so Gran had a "whip-round," raising enough money within the community to get Granddad into Pontefract Hospital to see a specialist.

The specialist concluded that Granddad's hipbone had been broken. Unfortunately it had now re-set itself - but in the wrong place. The specialist announced that the hipbone would have to be re-broken and re-set. If you are squeamish, look away now. Granddad was taken into theatre and laid on the operating table - on his good side. Fortunately, the specialist gave

Granddad a local anaesthetic, before cutting the flesh wide open. Granddad felt the large metal chisel being placed, scratchily, against his badly set hipbone. Out of the corner of one eye, he saw the specialist, with hand aloft, ready to swing the lump hammer down on the chisel head.

There was a sickening thud and crack as the lump hammer and chisel did their intended!

The outcome of the operation was eventually a success. Granddad could walk again. He now had one leg shorter than the other, and could only walk with a limp – but he could walk and he was alive. He would never again be fit enough to work *"darnt pit,"* and he never did! (Hooray!)

In addition to the awful and dangerous working conditions; both Granddads talked about the unfairnesses. One in particular was the way colliers were paid. The system for payment revolved around the "Motty Man". The colliers would hew the coal from the seam and then manhandle it into coal tubs. The tubs were small coal wagons that sat on metal rails, just the same as on the railways but with a smaller distance between the rails. The tubs were transported out of the mine through a combination of manpower and the miner's best friend (the pit pony). Then it went up and out of the mine via the lift, known as the "cage".

Each collier had his own identification number. The numbers were stamped onto metal disks for each miner.

When a tub had been filled to almost overflowing, the collier would hang one of his numbered disks onto the side of it – identifying that work as his.

The filled tub, accompanied by the collier's numbered disk (known as a "motty") was then sent back through the system and out of the pit. The man on the surface, checking the tubs of coal for both quality and weight, was called the Motty-Man. Now both Granddads were of the mind that the Motty-Men were a corrupt bunch. One of the Motty-Man's jobs was to determine how much each collier would be paid for each tub. Myth and legend had it that "friends of the Motty-Men" always seemed to have their tubs approved at a higher weight and quality, so they made more money. There was no transparency and fairness to the payment system. You got paid what the Motty-Man decided. That's "Awful Management".

Back in the 1920s private individuals owned the mines. It was not until "Vesting Day" on the 1st of January 1947 that the mines were nationalized. Against a background of poor working conditions, poor health and safety, unfair payment systems, and poor wages working for wealthy mine owners, the National Union of Mineworkers grew to be strong. The NUM were passionate in their quest for improvements in the lot of the colliers. Some would say that they became too passionate in their quest.

However in any system "Awful Management" leads to an oppressed workforce that will eventually push back!

Both Granddads came out of the pits in the early 1950s. Granddad Sheard borrowed money and bought a chip shop, then another, then sold them both, and bought a bookies – becoming a proper capitalist. However, on the other side of the coin, Mam's Dad (Granddad Bingley) had been an NUM representative during his time as a collier. Unbelievably he too came out of the pit and bought a chip shop. My Granddads didn't know each other at the time, so that was quite a coincidence.

Until retirement, Granddad Sheard remained a bookie. Granddad Bingley remained in his chip shop, but carried on with his political leanings and eventually became a Labour Councillor. The good news for me was that I was brought up balanced. I had one blue and one red Granddad. I could see that both had their good points! "Awful Management" does not listen to, or even consider, the other persons point of view.

Cows

Sometimes, during the long hot summer holidays, the peas weren't ready to pick. For a couple of days this would bring about a welcome change in proceedings. The farmer would corral half-a-dozen of us regulars for special duties. Sometimes we cleaned his vintage car collection, which we found really tedious and boring. Other times we were "wild oating" of the farming type, where you walk up and down a swaying field of corn pulling out "wild oats" by hand. We would clean out the ammonia ridden chicken houses, or our all time favourite - various intrusive veterinary duties with the cows.

Before a cow can be treated, one must first catch one's cow and contain it. The cows are not keen to be caught or constrained so, like everything in life, you need a process. Step one was to go out into the field full of cows, and in the absence of a sheep dog - be that dog. We walked slowly down the sides of the field, slowly surrounding the cows. Gently we would kettle them towards the gate and onward into the enclosed farmyard. Then the fun would start. We now had to coerce each cow, in turn, to walk down between the narrowing rails towards the cattle trap. The cattle trap held one cow at a time. Once in the trap, a bar came down behind the cow's head, trapping it. You could then do things to the beautiful animal – injections, painful removals of parts, breed continuation, eye drops etc.

For the young bullocks, there was added fun. Their young heads were too small to stay in the trap. The only way to contain them for "treatment" was for the six of us to restrain them physically against the wall leading up to the cattle trap. As we held the poor little frightened beast, the farmer would proceed to burn out their horn roots, or place a strong rubber band at the top of the testicle bag to stop blood flow and cause castration.

I must point out that these are standard farming procedures and that neither the bullocks nor the team got a mental kick out of it. Where any pain might be caused, the cows always received an appropriate anaesthetic. However the humans were kicked and butted on a regular basis. We were not anaesthetized, but we were skint.

One gorgeous blue-sky day there were no peas ready to pick. It was lunchtime and we were sitting opposite the cow trap some fifteen yards away. We had just had a morning of cows and we were bruised. It was hot, and we were thirsty and hungry. Thankful that it was lunchtime and we sat relaxed and tired, amidst the comfortable warm bales of straw. We dined under the cool shade of the barn canopy. One of the lads was about to bear down on his cheese sandwich. Just then, the Artificial Insemination man arrived in his van.

One of the techniques that cow breeders use, to see when a cow is ready for the AI man's charms, is to affix a dye plaster on to the rump of each cow. When the cows are at the "right time" their cow friends burst the dye plasters for them. The farmer sees the bright red dye on the back of the cow and immediately sends for the AI man. That morning we had seen a cow with red dye spread all over its back - hence the arrival of the AI man.

We put down our lunch and quickly set about the wrestling the freshly-dyed cow into the trap. Loud mooing and ferocious kicking ensued. Eventually the cow was in the trap - unharmed. Lucky cow! We all sat down, picked up our sandwiches, and got ourselves comfortable in anticipation of Act 2. This was real theatre in the round.

The AI man did "his thing" for a living. A few of us had previous experience of seeing his act. But there were some new boys in the team. They stopped in mid-chew as the AI man's arm disappeared into the back end of the cow. The new boys emitted "errrrrr" sounds, whilst the cow mooed a much-satisfied tune. It was at this point that the AI man said to the farmer, "Why are your cows always so bloody irritable and in a bad mood when it comes to getting them in to the cow trap? Do you only do bad things to them when they're in the trap? Don't you walk them through here regularly - so they don't just associate this place with bad things? Look at the cow now mooing away happily."

"Awful Management" brings the union representatives in to the management office only to give them bad news, or a "bullocking". No wonder they react so nervously to the invitation, and are already wound up when they arrive. For clarity, I'm not saying that our union brothers are cows: certainly not. What I am saying is that if you treat an animal or human badly, it learns and reacts accordingly...

***

I remember the late union leader, Vic Feather, addressing an audience of students in the University Hall, Aston, Birmingham. At the end of a very interesting, passionate, and witty hour-long speech, this working class hero faced his middle class opposites. He stood up at the front of the stage. He was short in height but massive in presence. Smiling at his young audience he whispered into the microphone, "Right you lot, if you ask a nice question, you will get a nice answer" – i.e. treat me nicely and I will treat you the same. People generally respond to you as you treat them and the more you treat them well, the more they respond positively to you!

The farmer took on board the AI man's wisdom. He stopped his own "Awful Management" ways and walked the cows through the yard and the open-ended cattle-trap every week. Sometimes he gave them tit-bits and sometimes he did have to "treat" them. Going to see the boss became a regular thing for them and their attitudes became more open and cooperative.

German unions

Back in the sixties English school children were brought up on the 3Rs: reading, writing and arithmetic. Now you may already be able to see a flaw in this approach. My proofreader certainly will. As a Yorkshire man, the Queen's English was not really my native tongue. English lessons did seem a little irrelevant back then. Second note to proofreader – English grammar and punctuation seem very relevant now. However, when it came to German lessons – no chance. I didn't understand English grammar, so how the hell could I learn German grammar? Plus, why should I bother with the language? - I would never go there...

Some thirty years later, I found myself working in beautiful Southern Germany. Unsurprisingly, most of the locals spoke excellent German. My American employers had just acquired a German family business. This manufacturing based company produced high quality extruded synthetic filament. The business was the town's largest employer and the Managing Director was effectively "Lord of the Manor" aced only by the Mayor. The factory lay at the side of the Danube, which glided slowly by shimmering in the hot sunshine – some five degrees warmer in the summer than back home. The Managing Director's office was on the first floor, with a balcony overlooking the Danube. A hundred yards upstream the narrow road bridge led up into the pretty medieval town.

I had arrived in this heavenly place due to some alcohol fuelled pool game in the States. My American employers had heard that yours truly could speak German. "Sheard had been taught German at school in England". Based on having sat in German lessons, not necessarily having learned German, I was clearly the obvious candidate for the job. In 1998, I started a new chapter of my management career. For the first time in my life, I had to manage people in a foreign land, using a foreign language, using different corporate laws, in a different culture, and with a very different approach to the unions.

Living in a country, you soon learn to speak the language. I was two when I learned to speak Yorkshire - and I couldn't yet read! However, the subtleties of language and culture take many years to learn.

I soon found out that the unions in Germany have some very big differences in approach, compared with their British counterparts. One reason for this is that a great deal of German industry was based on family owned businesses. This resulted in German Directors taking a longer-term view of investment and returns. The aim was to pass the business on to the next generation - not the next Venture Capitalist. Another trait of "Awful Management" is to ignore the longer-term. Noticeably, the German culture of planning longer-term had a very positive and stabilizing affect on employee union members. They felt the family owners were planning for the long-term, so giving everyone jobs for life.

One aspect of dealing with the German unions, which initially blew me away, was the fact that the union representatives have full access to every employee's record and pay level, with the exception of the senior Directors. German union representatives have to respect the confidentiality of these matters, in order to become a union representative recognized by the Union-Management Committee.

It is almost impossible to sack a German union representative except for breach of confidentiality. If they break this trust, even their mates will throw them out. This allows transparency and fairness in all matters of pay, training, and personal development. I always loved it that the management and the unions share the belief that development and improvement of individuals leads to development and improvement of the business.

The next surprise about German union representatives, which again completely blew me away, was how well trained they all are. In the UK we are now seeing more and more training of our management, thankfully. Typically it covers the basics of strategy, Profit and Loss, Balance Sheet management, Cash Flow management, Industrial Relations law etc. In Germany the union representatives were trained up to the same level as management on these business fundamentals. They were trained like us, they shared our information, and they often agreed with our direction and solutions, because they were engaged, informed and involved...

Years previously, back on the shop floor where the alleged b*****d had to be fired immediately without cause, things were different. I was out on the assembly department shop floor, casting my eye over the quality of workmanship on one of the electronic control cabinets currently being assembled. Some poor workmanship caught my eye. I immediately rounded on the assembler with a few sarcastic comments, supported by the local expletives, and officially proclaimed him as "stupid". This is a black-belt approach to "Awful Management". The victim sneered back at me, but begrudgingly said he would fix it. I had walked a few yards when one of the old timers politely asked me, "Gary, can I have a word?"

This true sage of life, the canteen, the pub, and factory floor pointed out that the gentleman I had just verbally speared was a human being. He had kids and a wife. They all loved him and doted on him. He was a qualified electronics engineer. He was certainly not stupid. Like most people on the shop floor he is capable of running his life, calculating winnings from complicated "flag bets" down at the bookies, running mortgages, and family economics. In short, most of them would respond in the same way as I would to the same information if you gave them it and took the time to explain it. So why don't you take a bit more time to explain what you want rather than shouting at people. Brilliant!

Now the very fact that the German unions were trained in understanding the business as well as the management led to a completely different dynamic. I was used to confrontation in the UK. Meetings with the German unions were all about how the business was doing, current issues, vision, what was required from the workforce to make it happen, and the training and development needed. In short, developing the people to develop the business. Awesome!

In the early days of working with the German unions, my use of the language slowed things down a little bit. By the end of my five-year sojourn, I was almost fluent and therefore dangerous. Remember what

Winston Churchill said, "When you think you understand the culture, you are dangerous." It is also true about the language. When you think you walk on water, you are about to sink.

The Germans are very house-proud and tidy.

At one meeting, it was stated by that, "As the major employer in the town, it is important that our buildings look clean, smart, and tidy". I was asked for fifty thousand Euros to repair the badger damage. When I questioned this, there was a long pause. I asked, "How are the badgers damaging the buildings, and do you normally have badgers so close to the river?" They looked at me and I looked back at them. Slowly the room filled with embarrassed laughter. If you look up "badger" and "roof" in the German dictionary - we had a problem with the roof not the badgers!

Every three months, I had to stand up in front of the German employees and their union representatives to give a full report on how the business was doing, its prospects for the future, and what would be required of the employees. These were lively affairs. At the end, everyone was well briefed. The quality of questions was high and mostly strategic in nature. By taking the time to get everyone in the boat, they were all sailing in the same direction. Thankfully, nowadays in the UK, this approach is adopted more and more. The sharing of information, engagement and involvement are becoming more and more prevalent. "Awful Management" could be under threat.

I enjoyed my five years in beautiful Southern Germany on the banks of the majestic Danube. There are some good lessons to be learnt from the German union's approach to management-employee relations, high level training of union representatives, and strongly aligning employee development and business development. To me the German model is based on a high level of respect for each other, experience, training, earned status, and position. I enjoyed working with the German unions. I mentioned earlier the balcony that overlooked the beautiful silvery Danube. The bloody mosquitoes showed no respect – "Awful Management"!

Chapter 3 "Awful Management" Checklist

1. Always provide poor working conditions.
2. Pay no attention to health and safety.
3. Do not be fair in you approach to pay.
4. Do not be fair in your approach to people.
5. Do not be tempted to train or develop people.
6. Give no time whatsoever to union or employee representatives.
7. Only meet the above to inform them there are "no pay increases".
8. Embarrass employees in front of their mates.
9. Share no company information other than closures.
10. Ignore other cultures and languages.

MARKETING

Chapter 4 - MARKETING

What is marketing?

I've never heard of a Marketing and Sales Director. The usual title is Sales and Marketing Director - putting the emphasis on sales before marketing. Which I believe is putting the cart before the horse.

When you ask what marketing is, people struggle to give a concise answer. Everyone has an intuitive feeling of what marketing is, but descriptions seldom come easily. Before giving the question my attempt, let's take a walk through a lively street market.

It's early morning. The stallholders have just arrived in their various types of worn and damaged transit vans. A stallholder dismounts from the driver's seat. Once outside, the first early morning cigarette is lit. The stallholder draws deeply and heavily on the abrasive, drug laden fumes. In the other hand a polystyrene cup of coffee is held firmly – purchased earlier from the local drive-through. The stallholders, each with their cigarettes lit, and coffee in hand, nod to their neighbouring stallholders (the competition), before flicking the cigarette end away, taking a final gulp of coffee, and then unloading the van.

Slowly and steadily, the vans are emptied of their various exotic contents. The produce is laid out in various arrays and formats. Some present their goods in jumble sale fashion - just strewn as a two-dimensional jumbled assortment across the wooden crosspieces. The more creative have brought their presentation stands with them, allowing a three-dimensional display to be created consisting of shiny apples, sun kissed oranges, and cauliflower brains amidst deep green leaves, and bright yellow bananas in curved intertwining patterns. Some of the stallholders display their prices on luminescent coloured cards sitting above the appropriate produce.

The market opens and the stallholders adopt various strategies to attract the now steadily building throng. Cries of, "Six oranges for two pounds - get your oranges." Other stallholders just stand there, hopefully, waiting to be asked, "How much is that?" The less hopeful stallholders stand there, talking on their mobile phones to some distant friend - while potential customers float past, unwilling to interrupt the call.

***

One of my favourite strategies is the guy with the large crockery stall. The expanded stall creaks with the weight of plates, pots, pans and silver like cutlery sets. He is accompanied by a couple of helpers. They stand at the front of the stand, ready to hand out goods to the lucky buyers. This showman stallholder starts. He juggles and clashes plates, accompanied with loud proclamations of, "I won't charge you twenty pounds, I won't charge you eighteen pounds, I won't even charge you fifteen pounds, give me ten pounds for the lot, who wants them?" The hands fly up. During such a pitch, it has been known for the performer to point to the back of the assembled throng and say, "Put your hand down Madam. Not yet." This indicates to the assembly that someone is willing to pay a high price for these quality items. The showman continues with his banter; the price continues to fall to the pre-determined level. The person with their hand up at the back is often an extraterrestrial - difficult to spot and quick to disappear. That's showbiz!

It is very unlikely that you would approach a stallholder before he or she had set out their stall. What *products* are they going to be selling? What will be the selling *price*? Which *place* in the market will they be setting up as their pitch? How will they be *promoting* their products? You have to set out the market place and understand it before you can sell. It is for this reason I would say that marketing comes before selling. The showbiz salesman couldn't perform until his market stall was set out. It's the same in business! "Awful Management" just goes out and sells without understanding the market.

So returning to the earlier question, "What is marketing?"

The basket of *products* that you sell, the *prices* that you charge for them, the *place* and market sectors you conduct business, and the ways in which you *promote* them are called the "*Marketing Mix*". One of the best definitions of marketing that I have ever read goes as follows...

Marketing is the optimization of the marketing mix for short, medium, and long-term profit.

The marketing mix
Products

Do you want to sell knitted fluffy alpaca cardigans to friends or passers-by dragged in from the wet streets? Do you have to sell sintered engine parts to the engineering buyers in the motor industry?

The answer to, "What products should we sell?" depends on where you are in the development and growth cycle of your business. If you are just starting out, then the question can be more a question of philosophy than accountancy. The sages say, "You should follow your heart," and "If your work is something that you enjoy, or you can make your passionate hobby the core of your job, the result is happiness and success." Wonderful stuff. However, the need to make a profit in order to sustain the business applies equally to an alpaca cardigan dream and a motor franchise.

If you are buying a product for £5 and selling it for £4 you will make a loss. It doesn't matter how many you sell. You will always make a loss. Spending more and more time and money on the marketing of the product and continuing to sell at £4 will - still make a loss. Surely anyone can see the wisdom of this argument, can't they? If the demand for the product continues, and you need to supply more and more product at £4, then you will have to go out and buy some more products for £5. At the same time, you are now taking more money out of the bank than you are putting in. Eventually you will have no money in the bank. Then nasty men will come round to your business, take all of your assets, desks, chairs, cars etc, close your business and send you home. You will have lost everything and feel depressed, due to your "Awful Management"!

This sounds so simple. Surely no one would ever carry on in business selling products for less than they cost? Sadly, they do. Why?

When you know the item costs £5 to buy, and you are selling it for £4, the data is clear. You can make an informed decision. For businesses making thousands of products, clear data comes from excellent accounting and computing systems. The costs involved in purchasing parts, manufacture, and delivery need to be gathered. All inputs need to be up-to-date, and communicated clearly to decision makers. These cost schedules are called "standard cost schedules". They should tell you, from start to finish, what any item costs to produce and deliver.

I remember working with a Newcastle client. All of the profit and more was spent on special deliveries to Cornwall. The special deliveries were needed to make up for time lost in manufacturing backlogs in the factory. The standard cost schedules showed that when the products were delivered to Cornwall by standard delivery, the business made a profit. The cost of special delivery put the supplied product into loss.

In manufactured products, the costs of raw materials, wastage, scrap, output levels, energy costs, and wages can all vary over time. It is therefore essential that all variables are kept up-to-date in the "standard cost" file. In an earlier example, the factory was doing everything it could to increase sales in order to fill the spare capacity of the newly acquired machines. However, the standard cost files showed that they would never make a profit. Sadly, the rest of the Team ploughed on in ignorance. The faster they went, the bigger the losses.

If you are in the alpaca knitted cardigan trade, the same rules apply. If the production and supply costs of feeding, shearing, spinning, knitting, selling, rent, rates, heating and lighting exceed the sales price, then you will lose money. Eventually you will run out of money and have to sell, or dare I suggest, eat all of those cute fluffy alpacas!

The simple aim is to sell the products that currently make a profit, or can be made profitable in the near-term. When you examine the "standard cost" file, there may be some products that are big losers, medium losers, and small losers. It may be possible, by better buying or production method improvement, to reduce the manufacturing costs of these products and put them into profit. Where there is no chance of getting large loss making products into profit, then they should be dropped immediately. Stop selling them!

At this point one often hears the Salesperson cry out, "But we need all of these products in the range, to supply the full basket of products that our customers desire." My usual reaction to this is, "Rubbish!"

I'm sure that Buyers would prefer the cheapest "one stop shop" in the west, but ninety nine times out of a hundred, they will simply "cherry-pick" your basket, and every other supplier, in order to get what they want, at the lowest possible price. They rarely have absolute loyalty to you, so you very rarely need to provide the whole basket of products.

It is the height of "Awful Management" to continue to supply products at a loss. Ignorance of standard costing methodology, or having out-of–date standard costings, is a road to disaster. You give more and more profit away. The sooner you can get on top of this problem, the better. With this problem behind you, the creatives within the business can look at expanding the product range, through either a wider sourcing of bought-in products or in-house product development.

Price

What prices should you charge for goods and services?

Again it depends on several factors. Are you a charity shop, a not for profit organization, a manufacturing based business, or an auction house? The fundamentals of the alpaca farm still apply. All organizations have bills to pay. The charity businesses may not have to pay the sales people, due to good people giving freely of their time. Nevertheless, eventually, even a charity shop will close if expenditure exceeds income.

There is something very exciting, primeval, and honest about an auction. Something is worth the price someone will pay for it.

A painting can be sold for millions of pounds, because someone was willing to pay that much for it. The standard cost of the paint, canvas, and the artist's labour, was but a fraction of the sales price.

In most circumstances, we would like to charge as much as possible for goods and services. Unfortunately, there are constraints on pricing due to competition (Dutch-auction, driving prices down), what people can afford, and as we have seen previously, the need to sell at a price above the standard cost in order to make a profit.

In most businesses, increasing the sales price has the largest positive effect on business profitability. That sentence is so important I will repeat it. *In most business, increasing the sales price has the largest positive effect on business profitability!* It is paramount customer facing members of the business know the best techniques for achieving maximum pricing. In a world of tendering on line, face to face selling is under pressure. But, going back to the street market analogy, it is always worth a look around the other market-stalls to see what prices they are charging.

You can always ask customers and competitors what prices they are paying or charging. Some will tell you, and some won't. Customers and competitors may even mislead you. Really? Unbelievable?

Something is worth what people will pay for it. Outside an auction, the only way to find out the price ceiling is to keep putting the prices up, until the customers won't pay any more. You may have to risk losing a couple of deals to find out the real maximum chargeable price. The better information you have on competitor pricing the better, in order to optimize your own sales prices. "Awful Management" has a habit of keeping poor standard cost files, and poor competitor information, leading to under pricing, losses, and a chance to get down the pub with a happy client.

One of Granny Sheard's favourite business stories was about when Granddad was still recovering from his broken (twice) hip. Whilst he was confined to bed, Granny was allowed by the pit owners to take an empty coal-sack down to the pit-yard and have it filled up with coal to keep the family warm. Granny, being the entrepreneur that she was, sewed two sacks together, making one enormous sack. At this point of the story Granny would have to sit down, as her eyes filled up with tears of laughter. The young gentleman in the pit-yard said, "Corr Missus, this is a big sack," as he draped it over the crossbar of the bicycle, ready for Granny's long push home. I guess the moral of this Yorkshire story is if it's priced at nothing people will take as much as they can.

There is an interesting correlation between the price people will pay for goods and services and their perceived quality. Granny was cute looking, short, and a good pusher of heavily laden bicycles. She was a cute businesswoman too. One of her favourite phrases was, "If it doesn't sell for a tanner, then put it on at a bob." (A tanner was six old pennies; a bob was twelve old pennies). Translated this meant that for certain crockery items, people won't buy them if the price looks too cheap. A higher price infers quality, and may have more appeal to a browsing potential purchaser. Cute!

***

Place

We have established the *products* and services to sell, and the *prices* at which to sell them. Next, where are we going to sell them, and how are we going to get them there? Or, put in marketing terms, what is our market place? What are our distribution channels?

Going back to our analogy of the street market, the *place* your market-stall sits within the market is important. It can greatly affect how many cabbages you sell. If your stall is facing where customers get off the bus, or come out of the car park, then they will see your stall first, and while their purses and wallets are full. Your chance of a successful sale is increased if people can actually see you in the market place.

There has been many a tussle, and alleged backhanding to the Market Manager, to get premium places on the market. The modern equivalent is paying a premium for the best key words, to improve your website listing position. Funny how the old method was seen as corrupt, and the modern approach is seen as "good profitable business".

I never felt that the guy at the back of the market, standing next to the Gents toilets, had a very good place. He stood there, with his suitcase open, full of cheese, black pudding, and ham. These were odorous surroundings. Not the place for selling delightful foodstuffs. His was an "Awful Management" decision. The *place* was wrong and I bought nothing.

On Friday nights, down at the local bustling and heaving pub, the cheese and black pudding man often visited us late into the evening. He wore his white butcher's coat, and carried a large wicker basket full to the brim with tasty goodies. It felt the right place to be buying cheese, ham, and bacon, at knock down prices. They were the very same products, but in a different *place*! After an evening of many beers, filled with good conversation, I have to confess after the two-mile walk home not all of the goods reached the family fridge. But I dropped into bed fulfilled and happy.

Mobile black pudding eating took place during my early years as a PhD student. After just one week as a postgraduate, I got married to my beautiful girl. Love may conquer all, but money pays the bills.

I was living on a student research grant, so I needed to find extra funds for the marital love-nest. So every quarter, having converted my grant cheque into real money, I set off over the mountains to Lancashire, to Manchester's wholesale jewellery district. There I would invest all of my 3 months grant money on watches, earrings, necklaces and the like. Upon returning to the marital mansion (2-bedroomed council flat), my young bride would "do her fruit." Then, in the classic "Yorkshire aggressive lady style," so excellently portrayed by Nora Batty in "Last of the summer wine" my blushing bride would ask, "What the bloody hell are you going to do with that lot?"

Around our local pubs, Thursday to Sunday tended to be the busy nights. Back in the seventies, it was common for "staff" to be paid on a Thursday. The shop floor Lads and Lasses were paid on a Friday. This meant there were four nights a week where people had money in their pockets, and many of them were "down the pubs" - my market *place.*

One of the "must have fashion items" for blokes was a Burberry jacket. This jacket had an incredible number of pockets - seventeen in total. With my jacket on, fully laden with stock, I was off to the pubs, four nights a week, flogging jewellery. The pubs were my market *place* and my jacket the market stall.

Looking back it was a risky enterprise. I was alone and had expensive goods in my pockets – although being six foot and fit may have dissuaded a few from having a go. There were no alarm systems on that jacket and the goods were not insured. My fast legs were the best security and insurance I had, but it was not a long-term, sensible approach to business. My approach to security and insurance were "Awful Management." I got away with it. Some don't.

Business in the pubs was good. I never had any trouble, except with rings. Pubs are the wrong *place* to sell rings. We humans are all different shapes and sizes. Rings are like shoes. You need a large range of sizes and styles when selling rings or shoes. That would mean holding a lot more stock. That's a lot more money tied up, not earning for you. If you are selling rings, you really need premises and a workshop at the back where you can make adjustments. So don't sell foodstuffs near the toilets, and don't sell rings in pubs. "Awful."

Can being counterintuitive sometimes work in your favour?

For many years, I did a constant round of international exhibitions, mainly around Europe and the USA. My Dad would interject at this point of the story with, "Better than working darnt pit, Lad," and he would be right. At the plastics shows you would typically see all of the machine manufacturers in their suits and ties, smiles at the forefront, brochures in hand, ready to pounce like panthers onto the nearest victim who blessed them with any eye contact.

All of the plastics manufacturers were at the exhibition. That is what you would expect. You would expect all of the car manufacturers at the car shows, computer manufacturers at the computer shows etc. However, a leather goods manufacturer realized all of the salespeople at these shows were busy all week. Their duties included being on stand, being in the bar and restaurant with clients, or being in bed for the three hours in between. This left them no time to get presents for the loved ones back home.

The leather goods people had the brilliant idea of not exhibiting at the leather goods shows - but selling at everyone else's! There in the middle of the car show would be a leather goods stall, packed with customers desperate to buy something to take home – a brilliant place to sell leather goods!

We have considered the stationary *place* to sell (a market stall), a permanent shop (a jewellers down the high street), being mobile (taking your goods around the pubs), or off-piste (selling at someone else's show). If you are a manufacturer, your market *place* could be the supermarkets, the sheds, or you may be a part supplier to other manufacturers. These are the traditional *places* to sell goods and services. In the last fifteen years, we have seen the rise of the internet as a virtual market *place*. "Awful Management" doesn't like change. It may be left behind in this rapidly changing *place*.

Promotion

Promotion here means to encourage sales of goods and services.

When it comes to *promotion* there is no substitute for putting yourself out there, meeting customers and prospects. This is not always easy. Some owners may be shy by nature - happier in doors, developing the next technological break through. Unfortunately, "Boffin based businesses" can die before they even get to market, or they may grow slowly, through word of mouth, between fellow "Boffins". I have seen these businesses accelerate rapidly by adding a marketer to the team. Once these "Best kept secret" businesses are known, they can fly. It is "Awful Management" to keep your light under a bushel.

The Czech Republic is beautiful country, with beautiful people and beautiful beer. It was August, at the turn of the century. We were attending an exhibition held where the original "Bud" beer comes from. The bustling city was drenched in sunshine. We were there for three days to *promote* our newly developed fishing line. This would be the first time we had exhibited in the Czech Republic. It was hot, I was nervous, but here we were in Ceske Budejovice, some 30 miles south of our Czech manufacturing plant.

The exhibition was just outside town, on an enormous site. The format was one I have never seen before. There were dozens of exhibition halls, peppered all across the site. These varied enormously in terms of size, shape and quality. In between the halls were trees and classic market-stalls, again of varying sizes. Roads, wide enough to take two cars, linked the halls and market-stalls. All roadsides were occupied by additional market-stalls and open-backed vans.

Every ten paces were hot-dog sellers or ice-cream vans. The whole place was hot, packed with stalls, a noisy, exciting, vibrant mixture of smells and sensations. You could buy anything, from a Combine-Harvester to a fake Rolex and a bag of sweets.

Our Czech Sales and Marketing Team were lovely people. We'd spent a lot of time together, and had some great nights out. However, *promoting* fishing line was new to them. When I arrived at the Exhibition Centre site, it was like looking at a scene straight out of the "Arabian Nights". I searched long and hard to try to find our exhibition stand. Becoming slightly desperate, I decided to phone our Czech Manager. Through the wonders of mobile telephony, and our common ability to speak German, he directed me to our exhibition stand - our *promotional* site!

Excellent – our site was central to the whole exciting gathering. We were on the intersection of five major roads. Dozens of potential punters were passing every second. Then, across a crowded intersection, I spied it - an old grey Portakabin. It had one door facing towards the moving masses, but the door was closed! It did have a small window facing the river of potential customers. The window was closed! The window was of the size and type where you would have to stoop to whisper, "Do you have any dirty postcards, please?" I knocked on the door and entered. The Czech Team shot up from their seats, giving me a warm welcome. I was immediately invited to take a not too shabby seat, and given a coffee.

The fishing line was all stacked neatly, in boxes, against the inside wall of the Portakabin. The product brochures gleamed in their racks. They stood erect, ready for any potential customer brave enough to knock on the door and ask, "What are you selling?"

I cried inwardly, cringing at the thought of spending the next three days in this awful Portakabin. We just had to get out there and *promote* this stuff.

You could get anything on this site, so we set about making a few purchases, from our impromptu *promotional* budget. We bought a couple sets of patio tables and chairs, along with sun umbrellas, fishing rods, bright fishing lures, and the star of the coming show – "Billy Bass!"

You may remember Billy Bass, the iconic singing fish. Billy plummeted kitsch to new depths. Billy wriggled and writhed as he sang, "Don't worry – be happy." Billy was eye and ear catching. Billy became our promotional saviour. Class or what?

We laid out the tables and other purchases in front of the Portakabin, adjacent to the roads filled with passing punters. The products were taken out of hiding and stacked on the tables. With fishing line now on show, the customers could touch it, feel it, and try to break it: the fisherman's favoured test. With our goods clearly on show, I sat discreetly to one side in the shade of an umbrella, pretending to be fishing with my newly acquired rod. I forgot to mention the new hat, of the Huckleberry Finn type, that I had purchased for maximum fisherman-look effect. Billy Bass was top, centre, and right at the front of our newly created market-stall.

The stage was set. Whenever any customer came near enough, I would gently lower the fishing lure in front of Billy's sensor. This would trigger Billy into action, writhing and wriggling to his thigh-slapping musical hysteria. Immediately the crowd would all stop. Some would smile, others would laugh, but many having stopped would come and have a look at what we were *promoting*. The sales team then moved in to close the deals. With Billy as our front man we immediately started to sell product. Morale lifted, and we had a cracking few days.

With Billy and a better presentational layout we had improved the on-site *promotion*. The 3 days proved that this was not the correct place to market high volumes of fishing line. The real route to market for volume sales was through the major distributors - which three days later is exactly where we re-directed the business.

Lessons were learned on that fun filled trip by getting out into the market place to see what was happening. The "Awful Management" approach to marketing is to stay in doors and guess where customers are, what they want, and at what price. Just like the Czech Sales and Marketing Team, cocooned in their Portakabin on that first morning. Once we got out there, meeting and talking to people, we learned a lot and moved forward quickly.

The highlight of the visit came towards dusk on the last day. Three busloads of Czech men were out for a day at the exhibition. By five o'clock in the evening, they were close to "Bud-saturation." As they slowly drew near to Billy I thought, "Shall I - shall I not?" Of course, I went for it. Billy did his stuff, lurching into his favourite song, but this time accompanied loudly by 150 very merry Czech men. They sang the song in English but with wonderful Czech dialect undertones. The first time through the song, it was great and really funny. Everyone sang and laughed. It was still great the tenth time through, until Billy's batteries finally gave in. A great moment in time, a fantastic memory was born of the need for *promotion*!

"Awful Management" would have stayed locked up, secreted away, in the bowels of that Portakabin. Hidden away from the potential customers, sales, market information, and all of that fun. No thank you!

Marketing and technology

Before the arrival of the internet, the main routes and technologies for connecting with potential clients were meeting people at trade exhibitions, advertising, hoping the telephone would ring, sending out mail shots, or cold calling. Hopefully a few prospects were gained from this work. You could then get into your car and hurtle off down the motorway. With mobile phones uncommon, your pockets needed to creak with the weight of silver coins to fuel the motorway services phones. There was always a queue at the motorway services phones, mostly outside. If you weren't on the phone, you were in the rain.

Today we are blessed with the internet, mobile telephony, and the opportunities for virtual meetings with customers anywhere in the world. All this can happen via the airwaves from the comfort of your own office, settee, or Board Room. The world of social media allows us to air our views and follow our inspirers at the dragging of a finger across a shiny hard screen. We should not forget there are real people at the other end! The technology may have changed, but people haven't. Technology can be a boon - but it can also bite you...

It's the early nineties. I've just carried out a successful mail-shot campaign. I'm on my way down the motorway to see a new potential customer. The traffic is very light. I'm cruising nicely along the smooth black tarmac, and "Born in the USA" is blasting out.

In the early nineties I was fortunate to have a car phone. These were big black bricks that sat between you and your front seat passenger. These phone barriers were allegedly invented to deter passenger-driver crossover - apparently possible in previous models.

At the top of the chorus, "Born in the USA," the brick rang, spoiling a tremendous solo. I turned off the car's cassette player and pressed the brick's green button. A threatening voice said, "Hello, is that Gary Sheard?" Highly trained, I replied, "Yes, this is Gary, how can I help?" The caller continued, "I've just received a letter from you lot, and at the top, it is addressed to, 'Dear does not pay his bills!"

Hearing this, my natural inclination was to burst out laughing. I realized this would be throwing fuel onto a glowing ember. I struggled to hold down my giggle valve for what seemed an age. Then simultaneously giggling and screaming I said, "I'm really sorry I'm laughing, I do take your call seriously, and I will fix your problem, but please give me a moment to compose myself. That is funny. But that is bad!" God bless him, his tone now changed, to one of embarrassed humility. He was brilliant, giving me another minute to sober up from my attack of the giggles.

It turned out that this agitated customer was a very slow payer. So slow, that when he eventually caught up and paid us everything he owed us, we had put him on pro-forma, so he had to pay in advance for any new orders before we would deliver them. At some point in his history, one of our administration staff had put a note on his electronic file, "Does not pay his bills." Somehow this comment was transferred electronically onto his mail-shot salutation. Amidst hundreds of other mail-shots it had sneaked out – only to bite us later in the bottom.

"Awful Management" forgets that customers are people. When you send out a letter, a human being will open it. When you send e-mail, there is a human being at the other end of it. When you post a blog, human beings will read it, and they all have different ideas and sensitivities. The majority of modern communicative technology is marvellous. I much prefer my mobile phone to standing in the rain, waiting my turn, for some urine-stenched phone box to spit out its last victim. So please be careful on the social media networks. It can take a lifetime to gain trust and one stupid comment to lose it.

The internet is fast becoming the marketeer's weapon of choice. There are now thousands of books on the subject of how to use it as your prime marketing tool, getting your website to attract potential customers, and the optimization of your website ranking through key words and search engines. This Christmas, 2013, I purchased 80% of the family presents on line. Ten years ago, I bought all of the presents at the shopping mall. The internet has changed the way we market and sell to potential customers. It will continue to change at a pace. It would be "Awful Management" to miss the wave.

Chapter 4 – "Awful Management" Checklist

1. Ensure standard cost files are not up-to-date.
2. Better still, don't have any standard cost files.
3. Be unclear which products make you money.
4. Charge what you can, even at a loss.
5. Never go out into the market place – you might learn something.
6. Promotion should be low key, but exhibitions are vital – socially.

SALES

Chapter 5 - Sales

Once we have the marketing mix established, it is the job of the Sales Team to optimize the sales and contribution to profits. The more of each profitable product we sell, and the higher the prices, the greater the contribution to profit.

Selling one item for one million pounds profit is better than selling one million items, each at a penny profit. We do not want to be busy fools. To prevent this, the Sales Department needs confidence in the company's standard cost files - knowing they are up-to-date, and that each sales price is high enough to make a profit. If the Marketing Department has armed the Sales Team with competitor price data, the Sales Team will be fully armed to sell both profitably and competitively, maximizing profit opportunity.

The wonderful world of selling is allegedly full of greasy snake-oil salesmen. Insurance sales types, people with double sided sticky tape on their bums, and estate agents sorts, with flash cars and the ability to talk straight through you. I'm sure some of this may be true, but the best sales people are highly trained, and completely focused on what might help the customer. "Awful Management" and awful sales people always focus on what they want, and not what the customer wants. A good sales person should be well trained and well armed, with the latest marketing collateral. More importantly they should be singing in their head, "If I can help somebody…"

Everything is a process: getting dressed, washing the dishes, making a car, making love, getting ready for work, going through the e-mail, cleaning the shoes, and even selling is a process. Thankfully, even within a well-defined process, there may still be room for flair and self-expression. Professional selling is a process, and in its simplest form, there are four clear stages:

Trust building - Building trust between you and the
customer.
Exploration - Exploring the customer's needs.
Testing - Testing understanding and possible
solutions.
Closing - Closing the deal.

The theory states that you begin by building trust. Once this has been achieved, and not before, can you then proceed onwards to exploration, testing, and closing. To be successful, each section must be thoroughly completed before moving to the next.

Gaining trust

In the mid-eighties, I had just been promoted to Local Director of a management consultancy practice. I had to generate sales and a profit. Selling consultancy is quite different from selling jewellery round the pubs. In management consultancy, you don't actually have a product to sell. You are selling an approach, a service, which may result in some unquantifiable benefits later. When selling management consultancy you are meeting people for the first time. When selling down at your local pub, people already know you. They also know what you are selling, your other customers, and your reputation.

In my early months as Local Director, I was finding that out of every four customer visits, only one would sign up. Now I know that I'm very loveable, nice, well intentioned, and that we could deliver some great improvements for customers, but my sales success rate was not good enough. It was at this point that our inspirational leader sent me on a training course that changed my life.

The course was based on a matrix.

(See later illustration – Inter-personal styles matrix).

A couple of weeks before the course started, I received half-a-dozen sealed envelopes. Unbeknown to me at the time, these envelopes contained forms to be completed by family or friends. Each form listed a hundred questions about my interpersonal style.

The forms were completed, away from my prying eyes, and returned to the training course organizers. I never got to see the malicious, un-informed, malevolent, how could they possibly know contents. A few weeks later, thirty other victims and I arrived at the training centre. The set up was unique: a combination of southern pub, hotel and training centre. A great combination when you are in your mid-thirties.

The two days were a heady mixture of psychology lectures, role-play, feedback, drinking, and eating to excess. We tried to solve all the problems of the world until five in the morning, while continuing to drink. We felt moderately superior to others around us, slouching on a settee, with our arguments built on moving sands.

At the end of the first day, you understand the Matrix. The horizontal axis shows some people are natural tellers and some are natural askers. The vertical axis shows some people are naturally poor listeners and some are naturally good listeners...

INTERPERSONAL STYLES MATRIX

poor listeners

ANALYTICALS	**DRIVERS**
Ask	tell
AMIABLES	**EXPRESSIVES**

good listeners

The matrix shows there are four basic types of inter-personal styles:

Driver listeners	Natural high tell	Naturally poor
Analytical listeners	Natural high ask	Naturally poor
Amiable listeners	Natural high ask	Naturally good
Expressive listeners.	Natural high tell	Naturally good

The original course came from marriage guidance counselling in the USA. The concept is that we all have to sell. This may not be a product. It may be an idea. In our daily home and work lives we are all always trying to sell our ideas or persuade others. The key is to understand how we like to be dealt with, then work out how the other person likes to be dealt with, and then move to each other.

Now each quarter of the matrix can be sub-divided. So if you take the bottom left quarter of the Driver box you have an Amiable-Driver, top left quarter of the Driver box is an Analytical-Driver, top right of the Driver box is a Driver-Driver, and bottom right of the Driver box is an Expressive-Driver. This method of sub-division can be applied to each of the four primary quadrants to get the right nomenclature.

I'm glad that bit's over with. At the end of the first day, the analysis of our "friends" form filling were unleashed upon us. Prior to our arrival, the forms were fed into the computer, and the answers had come back. I was an Expressive-Driver, and with little flexibility. I questioned myself, "How could that be so?" How could my friends say, "He loves to showboat, domineering, not one of natures naturally good listeners, approaches everyone the same!" Although the good comment was, "He likes to do things and get things done."

I thought, "I'll do them when I see them!" How could they possibly get me so...so...so...right as it happened? The second day of the course gave hope to even the most "Awful Management" inter-personal stylists!

***

The most personable people, and the best salespeople, have the "flexibility" to move towards the style of the person they are talking to. They can speed up their conversations when talking to the Drivers. They can talk more about the details when in the company of Analyticals. They can talk about family and soft stuff with the Amiables of this world. They can leave their egos in their pockets when talking to the arm flailing, self-centric Expressives.

"Flexibility" was our major theme on day two of the course. We learned that poor communicators, and poor sales people, tended to have low inter-personal flexibility. We were then given our results for inter-personal flexibility, based on the evil form filling of our ex-friends back home. Highly flexible people would score five, low flexibility people would score one, and with shades in between. I naturally expected to score high. I opened the envelope and looked at my score. It was a big – one - OUCH!

The good news was over time you can work on your flexibility, and improve your score. Once you learn that we all have different styles, and like to be interacted with in different ways, then the door to interpersonal improvement opens. One of the areas I needed to work on was my listening skill. On the scale of one to ten, where ten is a good listener, I was a four: not a catastrophe, but room for improvement. If you remember nothing else from this section, I suggest you highlight these following words:

To become a better listener - give the other person more eye contact!

Now please don't leer at the other person and end up on a disciplinary warning, or in a police cell, but just try it, gently at first.

Giving more eye contact has two effects. Firstly, because you are now looking at the other person, you will pay more attention to what they are saying. Secondly, the fact that the other person now sees that you are interested in what they are saying motivates them to continue, and with more openness and quality.

I said earlier, before going on this course my sales conversion rate was in the lower quartile. After the course, my sales conversion rate started to rise steadily as I became more and more competent in the techniques I'd learned. Selling to Drivers was fairly natural for me. These were the "wham bam thank you man" people blessed with the same interpersonal style as myself.

Before I went on the course, I thought that everyone was like that. Wrong! I had immediately excluded, and alienated, seventy-five per cent of my potential audience. The course had taught me to give more eye contact to everyone, and so focus and listen better. The course had also taught me to spend more time on detailed preparation before meeting Analyticals, talk about soft stuff first when meeting with Amiables, and not to talk about me when dealing with the ego-centric Expressives. With these adjustments to my approach, six months after attending the course my sales conversion rate was in the third quartile!

A year after attending the course, we all returned for a day's review and to see how our flexibility scores had moved. My embarrassing low score of one had raised to an incredible four out of a potential top mark of five. My interpersonal flexibility was now, as judged by others and not me, a highly flexible four. The rationale given for this impressive move was that although our attitudes are usually firmly established by the age of seven, our behaviours can be modified over time, particularly where we see a benefit. I had seen the benefits of moving towards people and being a good listener. When I look into my darling wife's eyes and listen, a good evening follows. When I don't – let's not go there!

The realization that we all have different interpersonal styles, and learning how to use this knowledge, was a great stepping-stone in my own personal development and career. Up until this point, I had thought that, "Everyone thinks like me." This self-centric thinking can be at the very heart of "Awful Management". Management shouldn't be about the Manager – it should be all about what the Manager could do for his or her people. Trust can be gained more easily when the other person believes you are there to help them and not yourself.

The course did change my life. My sales increased. More importantly, the quality of my relationships improved, both at home and at work. There is a lot of great reading on this subject. "How to win friends and influence people," by Dale Carnegie, is the natural accompaniment to the interpersonal styles course approach. I highly recommend giving it a good read.

Exploration

There is a big difference, in terms of the trust and screening required, between selling products for a military contract and oranges from a market stall. With potential sales to the military, there will undoubtedly be pre-screening of your business, and maybe you, even before you set off for a sales meeting. Assuming that we have arrived at the customer's premises, and had the introductions, tea or coffee, chocolate biscuit, ascertained the relevant elements of personal history, football team preference, and attained a level of trust. We now glide into the exploration phase.

"Awful Salesmanship" says to the customer, "You need one of these," even before ascertaining what the prospective customer's business is all about, and what they perceive their needs to be. The exploration phase is all about asking as many relevant questions of the customer as possible. After the pleasantries, a good opener is, "Please can you tell me all about your business?" Nowadays, you should know a lot from the customer's internet site before meeting them. This good opening question can be followed up by the whole gambit of who, what, why, where, when, how, and anything else?

At this point in the sales process, you have built a workable level of trust, and you are digging to find out what is really needed by the prospective customer. Up to this point, don't even think about getting your sales presenter out of its case. Quite often, the pre-meeting thoughts of both you and the customer are not where you end up.

I remember my very first consultancy job, high in the hills above a grey rainy Sheffield. The brief from the customer was to look at all the transport delivery schedules and see if they can be improved by re-scheduling. I spent a week trying to get to the bottom of the issue. I remember the lunchtime sandwiches had a plethora of beetroot on them. I like beetroot when it's lightly pickled, but this was straight from mother earth. Not nice. I worked away at the schedules, all on my own, in a grubby back office. Quickly I became frustrated, bored, and self-doubting.

I then had a flash of inspiration. Beetroot can do that to you.

As a Manager, my approach was to get out onto the shop floor and ask the lads, "What's going on, what do you think the problems are, and have you any thoughts or solutions?" Turning up as a consultant had conditioned me to behave differently. It was my job to be solitary, really clever, and to turn up smart. But this approach was getting me nowhere. "Awful Management" sits in offices away from the problems, hoping they will go away.

After half an hour with the lads on the shop floor, it became clear that there was no real problem with the existing schedules. After a week looking at them I had reached the same conclusion. The real issue was low morale, due to poor Industrial Relations. There were no regular meetings between the Managing Director and the Union Representative, so the lads never felt engaged. The level of trust between them and the owners was low. Completely "off brief," I suggested that chairing a joint "clear the air meeting" between Management, union, and other shop floor representatives. The outcome was agreement to a monthly business update and consultative meeting.

It turned out the Managing Director was new in the job. He had previously been an accountant and thought the answer to his morale problem was somewhere in the numbers. My boss, the guy who had sold the consultancy project, was a former production engineer, and also thought the answer was in the numbers. He had not found out the real problem before pitching a solution. The real problem was industrial relations, not transport schedules. "Awful Management" had not asked the lads on the shop floor, "What do you think the problems are, and have you any ideas for solutions?" The salesman had not taken enough time to explore deeply enough what was really wanted.

Testing

Hopefully, we now have the customer's detailed view on issues and needs. It is now your turn - and not before!

You can take out your samples, kit bag, presentation, laptop, pad, or whatever means of marketing promotional collateral you feel appropriate. You can show, tell and test away to your hearts content, or as time allows.

The magic questions at this stage are:

"How do you feel about that?"

"Is that what you had in mind?"

"Are we getting closer now?"

All the time you are testing the appropriateness of potential solutions. You are testing and being helpful. The probability of making the right product or service offering is increasing as a function of presentation and testing time.

This part of the selling process is where you get to listen to and overcome the customer's objections - if you really can overcome their objections, you get to pitch your Unique Selling Points (USPs), and you get to do your presentation. Again, there are many great books devoted to each of these key elements. But for me it's smiling, lots of eye contact, lots of listening, being honest, and being well prepared.

To start your presentation by rummaging through a kit bag, looking for power sockets, and asking the customer for other presentation equipment will lose you an opportunity. Before the advent of laptop presentations, there was a famous story of a presenter using slides and carousel projector. Just after starting a too many slide presentation, the fan inside the projector broke. The presenter then had ten seconds to show each slide before the heat of the bulb melted the slide, and the projected image swam to the sides of the screen.

You have built trust, you have explored the background and the needs of the prospective customer and you have suggested and tested various answers, solutions, products or services to fill the yearnings of this needful human being. It is now time to move from foreplay to the climax of the sales process.

Closing

Your company may have spent months on researching and reviewing the market place, and producing the appropriate high gloss marketing collateral and sales material. The Sales Team has been on the training course, with five nights stay in London, and as much beer, wine, and food, as a person with a mouth can consume.

You have got up early, zoomed down the motorway with phone in one hand, sausage roll in the other, and the Lucozade between the knees, only the thumb of the right hand and opposing finger gripping lightly on the wheel (all absolutely not recommended, and based on hearsay) – all designed for this moment – the "close".

You pull into the car park and secure the very last parking spot.

You brush the crumbs from the driver's seat and your bottom. You check your tie (gentlemen) and hair (ladies and gentlemen) in the window of the car, check the flies are up (trouser wearers) and pocket flaps out, and with a rub of the toe caps (I give up) behind the trousers, you stride up the path and into reception - full of enthusiasm and anticipation...

While in reception, please allow me a short digression. I have found there is a direct correlation between the quality of the reception area, the tidiness of the Managing Director's desktop, and the performance of the business. "Awful Management" allows the reception area to decline with age. This attitude to untidiness at the front of house continues through the business, eventually resulting in business problems.

You wait ten minutes in reception. Your prospective future friend, and customer, comes down the stairs to greet you. After a hearty welcome, the obligatory discussion about the traffic and the weather ensues. You walk to the meeting room – a room kept especially cold and barren for alien types. You sit. A hot drink is sometimes summoned. You wait until the right moment, then gently nudge the conversation down the track of trust, explore, test and something else?

The meeting ends. The morning's journey goes into fast reverse. You want to get home in time for tea, to see the family and one of the stars of Coronation Street who is about to get their just deserts. But wait a minute - that's a disaster. You never asked for the order. You never closed!

The fourth element of our sales process quartet is called the "close".

All the hard work before the meeting, and the meeting itself, aims at helping the prospective customer become a real purchasing customer. In order to do this, you have to close the deal. You have to ask for the business, the order, the signed contract etc. However, if you ask a straight question - you may get a straight answer. Not asking at all is worse – it is "Awful Salesmanship". You have wasted a large piece of time, money, effort, and not carried out the task you went to do. The subject of closing is, as you would expect, well covered on the internet. There are hundreds of ways of closing.

The most basic close is to ask the potential customer, "Can I have an order please?" A problem with this direct question is the answer can be yes or no. The art of closing is to reduce the probability of a no answer.

To improve the odds of a yes, many approaches to closing have been developed. These range widely in their guile, cunning, and manipulation. Some are on the borders of ethicality. I will give you a few examples here, and your soul is your own. A well-used car-salesman close is called the "blue-red" close. Imagine at the end of the smiles, the coffees, the endless forms, the walk around the site, the test drive, the relief at using their toilets, the car-salesman finally closes with "Will you be taking the blue car, or the red one Sir?" The question assumes no is not an answer, so the risk is reduced. He now has a higher probability of success - a deal.

The simplest of closes is called the "baby close." Parents will recognize this one, and those of us who have been children!

The torment goes like this:

"Dad can I have an ice-cream?" "No," replies Dad.

"Dad can I have an ice-cream?" "No," replies Dad.

"Dad can I have an ice-cream?" "No," replies Dad.

"Dad can I have an ice-cream?" "Have a bloody ice-cream," replies Dad. Dads can be wonderful people.

One of the closes that you won't find listed I've called "The Ditherer's close". I can't say that I developed this one. It was more a case of stumbling over it, by accident. I was over in Lancashire trying to help, a prospective client by selling some business improvement consultancy. I had gone through the sales process by the book, building trust, exploring his needs, testing possible approaches with him, but every time it came to closing and agreeing a deal he would go back to the exploring phase. After three hours of being on my best behaviour, I finally snapped and spurted out, "You're a ditherer aren't you?" He replied snappily, "What, me, a ditherer? No!" Within a fraction of a second, he stood to his full height and puffed out his chest. He announced loudly, to me, and all of the office furniture, "The project will start first thing Monday morning!" That's closure.

We all have different hot buttons and triggers. Being accused of dithering was certainly that gentleman's. It was my job to ask for the business, and we certainly helped him move things along during the following months. You have to believe in what you are selling and I did. I knew he needed help and I new we could help him. You have to be true to yourself in selling and helping. Trust, explore, test, close and then you can go home! So I did – no dithering.

Sales Management

I love sales people - socially!

To manage them can be a nightmare. They are the robins, the magpies, the sparrow hawks, the parrots, the gannets and the penguins of the business world. They can fly off into the air at a moment's notice, they can dive for cover at the merest threat of questioning, and if not disturbed from their flow then they can go on and on and on talking. They are wonderful people! No sales people, no sales, no business.

One morning I set off early to see a customer based on the outskirts of Bristol. On a good day this can be a five-hour drive from Yorkshire. My Sales Manager had said, "This is an important customer, and well worth meeting." I was a new Managing Director, keen to get around and meet our main customers. I drove on through the dark, yawning as I went, and gradually wakening. The dark, shiny, wet, black motorway, glided underneath my car-bonnet.

After five hours driving, stopping for pit stops, and three or four CDs later, I arrived at the customer's car park. There my Sales Manager met me. After the customary greetings, we went in to see the customer, an old friend of my Sales Manager. We sat, had coffee and biscuits, the two of them talked and joked, and raptured on about the old days and nights out at exhibitions on the continent. I observed and listened, and started to worry a little bit - well a lot!

"Awful Management" within sales management has many forms. The customer was a best friend of my Sales Manager. The Manager had wanted to show me how good his relationships were with customers - how "bon" his "bonhomie" was with key people in the industry. In short - what a thoroughly good chap he was.

The problem was this customer spent very little with us, and when he did spend, we made no profit. The journey had cost us hundreds of pounds in time and petrol and gave nothing in return. An awful waste – "Awful Management."

Sales people have higher than average salaries and bonuses, they have high expense costs, and they are "out of sight and mind" for their Managers. They need motivating and managing more than most. Being sensitive flowers, it is better that they are trained to manage themselves, as they tend to respond poorly to direct management. Given good training, business understanding, motivation, marketing collateral, and direction - sales people can be moved from sulky darlings to mega-stars!

It is well documented that sales people can be categorized into two basic groups: "Hunters," who go out and get new business, and "farmers," who look after existing business. One of my Sales Managers was a "farmer". He was quite happy to go out and look after existing accounts, but unhappy to go out looking for new business. In most businesses, there is the need for both types of activity. "Awful Management" doesn't know the hunters are looking for "small-game" and the farmers are standing in small fields, smoking. It won't know because it doesn't ask for monthly visit plans, visit reports and sales statistics.

An excellent sales team is a blessing, a "must have" in any business. To achieve this you need a combination of good, well trained people supported by a good marketing team, good marketing and sales collateral, a bonus scheme based on increasing the profit contribution, good reporting and regular reviews. Any less would be truly "Awful Management!"

Chapter 5 – "Awful Management" Checklist

1. It's relationships that matter - not higher prices and more business.
2. Only employ people who have comedy skills in sales.
3. Never train sales people - they may become a threat.
4. Let sales staff vent their feelings on the internet.

COST MANAGEMENT

Chapter 6 - COST MANAGEMENT

Mr Charles Dickens was quite right about income and costs...

Earning more than you spend can lead to happiness. Spending more than you earn will lead to misery.

It is the job of every Managing Director/CEO/Executive Chairman/Owner to make sure expenditure does not continually exceed income – a fundamental to the continuation of the business. To do any less is "Awful Management".

Within most businesses and organizations the major areas of cost are employees, purchases, distribution, utilities, rent & rates, depreciation and finance costs. All of these costs have to be funded from sales - made by those wonderful people in the Sales Office, or out on the roads in their BMW hot rods. However, even if you have managed to achieve great sales results, be sure not to "burn" the business through poor control of spending. "Awful Management" loves uncontrolled spending.

Employee costs

What is a business? It is people doing stuff towards a common aim. If you work in the Public Sector, your common aim is that of the department you work in. If you work in the Private Sector, your common aim is to make a profit to fund your future. The Public Sector is funded by taxes raised directly or indirectly from the

Private Sector. So, whatever your politics, we need profitable companies that can re-invest for the future, and we need great public services to look after us all. The size of the cake (taxes), and how to cut up the cake (government), ultimately rests with the voters. Whether we are talking about personal, family, corporate, or government finances – Mr Dickens is still right. You can't keep spending more than you earn. "Awful Management".

One of my mentors once said, "If I could run a business without bloody people, I would!" This outburst was the release of frustration from many dealings with the Human Race. We are all different, thank goodness, all with our different ways and traits - but also with different skills. At one level, we are spiritual ethereal beings. At another level, we are quite simply a cost.

"Awful Management" will not have the right number of motivated people, in the right places, and at the right level of pay. So what is the right number of people?

The answer starts with, "What is the vision?"

Followed by, "What are the plans to achieve the vision - on a month by month departmental basis?"

Then, "What organizational structures are required - to deliver the plans?"

This leads to the preparation of detailed staffing plans - right down to the positions and names of every employee. This process will determine the initial manning levels at a high level. To determine the number of people needed in detail, there is no substitute for "process-mapping". Everything is a process.

One of the best examples of the benefits of process mapping is to compare the old "typing pool" method of letter production with today's PC or laptop process. Back in the seventies the manager would hand write his draft letter. Eventually the secretary would come and pick it up from his out tray. Some days later the secretary would re-appear, with her draft typed copy of his letter. She would place it in the manager's in tray. The manager would eventually get around to checking and amending it, before putting it back in his out tray for the next draft to be prepared. A week later the letter was ready to go out. What a long process!

Today we can type for ourselves. The built in spell and grammar checker does its job at light speed. We can attach the letter to an e-mail in seconds, press the send key and it's gone. No envelopes or stamps are needed, and nor is the typing pool.

When looking at staffing levels in detail, it is important to look at each position through the eyes of a process map. Once you have a process map for each area or function, examine each element of the process by asking: who, what, why, where, when, how, else? The outcome of this work should be a more efficient process, and the correct allocation of staffing levels. Employees cost money. It is the job of management to ensure that only the right numbers of staff are employed, neither too many nor too few, and that they are using the most efficient, affordable processes available.

When I first worked in Eastern Europe, the approach to setting manning levels could be quite different to Western thinking. They were just emerging from communist rule, where the well-meaning aim was that everyone should have work. Unfortunately there was not always enough meaningful work for everyone. You could find people employed to, "Check the work of the Checker's Checker's Checker!"

One great quote defines hell as, "The place where you play football all day but there are no goalposts." The morale in the Eastern European factories that I saw was never high - until we injected some goals, aims and rewards. Then our fellow human beings were just as good as we were when encouraged and allowed to show their true talents. Sometimes they were better. "Awful Management" does not set goals and targets for its workforce, it allows its people to work in hell, playing football or hockey all day, but not supplying any goal posts.

There is a constant need to review manning levels in a business or organization. Demands and needs change, so the numbers, quality, and category of people needed are constantly changing. We have already discussed the need for clear organizational structures, goals, targets, reviews, personal training, and development plans. We also need to make sure we are paying enough – but not too much. Here the Human Resources Department (HR) needs to do its stuff. Internally we need to ensure that people doing the same job are paid the same money. Externally we need to be aware of the salaries on offer for equivalent roles.

In one German company, it became apparent that if you were a friend of a certain Director you were on a higher salary than your colleagues. I have seen the same situation in Yorkshire. In both cases, the "Awful Management" practice was stamped out as soon as it came to light. It should never have happened in the first place.

So far, we have looked at getting the staffing and pay levels right. In an earlier section, we looked at "vision" as the engine of motivation. But what do you pay for a Georgie Best, a Maggie Thatcher, a Vic Feather, or a modern Superstar?

You could take the view that a high cost employee is really an investment. If they are going to give a big return on that investment, then so be it, even if the salary looks high relative to the majority. Actually every employee is an investment. We should only be employing new people in a business if they will increase the profit. Likewise, we should only be letting people go if that will increase the profit of the business.

"I want you to sack that bast***!"

The heart-felt appeal from a former boss as he glared into the eyes of the Shop Steward – "Awful Management" in its finest form. Back in the early eighties, employment law was slowly balancing the rights of employees and employers. It was still pretty easy to "get rid" of a troublesome employee. The penalties for "unfair dismissal " were not severe. Today, thankfully, managers cannot dismiss employees purely on a whim.

Whenever asked, "Should we 'get rid' of someone," my approach is always the same. Firstly, "Is the role redundant and why?" If it is a true redundancy situation, caused perhaps by lack of work or changing working practices, then there are well-documented procedures to go through. Today these procedures are all on line and there is no excuse to ignore them. "Awful Management" ignores them at its peril. There are no short cuts. Secondly, where it is not redundancy but alleged under-performance or poor fit, I ask these questions:

Did we clearly define the job specification before the job interview?

Did we carry out more than one interview before appointment?

Did we have potential colleagues present in those interviews?

Did we check out the references before appointing?

Have we set out a clear job description with goals and targets?

Have we monitored performance and given feedback?

Have we documented all this?

Have we highlighted any training issues and dealt with them?

Having done all of this, have we seen any improvement?

If we have seen no improvement, have we now started formal performance management, and is the employee clear that they may lose their job?

Only when all of this has been carried out can you let an employee go.

Purchasing costs

In the majority of businesses, the quickest way to improve profits is to increase sales prices. In businesses involving the processing of raw materials, the second quickest way to improve profits is to reduce purchase prices. The Purchasing Team can greatly influence the profitability of a business - and yet "Awful Management" has a habit of undervaluing this critical function. A good buyer can create as much profit for you as a good sales person. Good buyers need to be cherished just as much as a good sales people.

Purchasing, like everything else, is a process. The buyer fires into action after the product specifications have been agreed with the customer, the engineers or product development people have signed off the product specifications, and a works order has been placed with the purchasing department. Then, and only then, can the buyer look where to place a purchase order.

If you ever ask your wife, husband, partner, best friend, "What would you like for Christmas," and they respond, "Just get me something nice," the probability of getting it right is small. You are doomed to failure. If vague requests are placed on a buyer, don't be surprised if you receive something different from what you had pictured in your head. It is after all your head, and not the buyer's head. Requests such as, "similar to last time, only just a bit bigger," will result in tears, arguments, lost time and eventually lost customers. These are actual "Awful Management" requests.

When it comes to sourcing, the buyer's mantra is quality, price, and delivery. The buyer wants quality assured products, that meet the required specification, at the best possible purchase price, delivered on time. I would add a fourth element to the mantra: best possible payment terms. This means being allowed a longer period of time before payment is due, or discounts for early settlement.

So the buyer's mantra is: quality, price, delivery, and terms.

There are pluses and minuses to consider in any new negotiation with well established suppliers. Where quality is paramount, such as in jet engine turbine blades, changing supplier to achieve a small saving per blade is a high risk strategy. Having a second alternative source is still important.

Suppliers are human, and they will at some point let you down. You therefore need quality alternatives, approved and tested to the same level as the main supplier's products. It's also important that your suppliers know you have options. This gives you a stronger negotiating position. "Awful Management" has no alternative suppliers, and is going to be paying too high a price until it has no money to pay.

What price should you pay?

If you have a list of quality-approved suppliers, you can ask for quotes, and carry out a "lowest price gets it," Dutch Auction process. Invariably, due to poor planning and control, "Awful Management" will need the goods right now. Therefore they won't have time to complete a "Dutch Auction" process, and will want to by-pass the process, paying for the privilege. We are in business to make money. Giving buyers time to do their jobs in full is a key part of keeping costs down – and profits up.

An old friend had been a senior buyer within the UK car industry. His view on suppliers was, "You can't just keep screwing down suppliers to the lowest price - 'like wot these young-uns do'. Sometimes you have to do your suppliers a little favour or two. Then in times of shortage, those suppliers that you had looked after will look after you. Your competitors, with the young buyers, will run out of supplies before you do."

A counter argument is where close relationships have existed for some years between a buyer and seller, the commercial outcomes are not being optimized. With this in mind, it's recommended to shuffle the pack every couple of years. An alternative approach is, as the Russians so beautifully put it, "Trust but audit." Through regular auditing, make sure your buyers are following internal procedures, and they know about regular internal audits. Similarly, where your senior sales people have long-standing relationships with key customers, make sure you do the occasional joint visit! "Trust but audit" and find that "Awful Management."

To "Awful Management" ignorance can be bliss. Unfortunately, in heavily contractual business, "The Devil is in the detail." It always pays to look at the detail in the small print when purchasing. The apparent low price offered may not be so good when you dig into the detail. You have to dig and compare to get the real "best price".

If your buyers don't like detail, then soon you won't like them. "Devils in the detail" to watch out for on quotations include plus transport, volume discount does not apply, price available until, plus local taxes, etc. When carrying out your analysis of quotations, consider all of these elements to determine the best deal.

Every employee is part of the organizational body. Just like a human body, all parts are connected. The buyer has to be aware of the blood flow (cash flow) available at any time within the body of the business. Good deals are often available for volume purchases, but that is no good to the Finance Director if cash is tight. It would be a crime to spend all of the company's money on a large order for volume-discounted nuts. If cash is getting tight, the Finance Team need to keep the Purchasing Team informed how much cash is available. This can be on a daily, weekly, or monthly basis, depending on how far "Awful Management" has let the situation develop.

Buyers have always been potential targets for corruption.

Business trips to the South of France, trips on large shiny powerboats, Grand Prix, high quality hotel stays at the weekend, fine wines and dining, Christmas gifts, holiday flights etc. This was the stock in trade of the eighties and nineties. This is how the wheels of industry, and potential buyers were, allegedly, influenced. If everyone is doing it, is it wrong? First test – "Law of the land," second test, "What is the local culture?"

In the Middle East it is still "custom and practice" to buy the potential customer a gift. Every potential supplier does, and you all know that is how business is done. It is not corrupt - because it is a level playing field. Now when is a bribe not a bribe? I guess it depends on the local culture and the laws of that land. In the UK today, I think the pendulum has swung too far on the side of caution. When you can no longer buy suppliers, or customers, a coffee without it being construed as a bribe – that's awful.

Having purchased your goods, it is essential to check that you got what you ordered. The next step is to check you were charged correctly for what you received. "Awful Management" will assume that everything is all right. Again, "Trust but audit" is the order of the day. The more trust you gain with a supplier, the less you have to audit.

The fundamentals to check upon receipt of a delivery are quantity and quality. There are many ways that through accident, bad intentions, or poor processes, you can be diddled, robbed, mugged, screwed, turned-over, and cheated on the supply side!

Remember the pea-pullers? They would hide mud, stones and bricks in the centre of the pea-sacks. We were paying for weight – ceramics, dirt, and water weigh more than peas. There are variations on this trick to watch out for where payment by weight is involved. One classic concerns trading waste paper. It is amazing what affect a stray hosepipe can have on a skip full of waste paper.

Where cases of goods on pallets are involved, it is amazing how often the "case mouse" can devour a whole case - usually from deep within the pallet load of cases. It is interesting that the guys who collect the broken pallets always start taking the good pallets first. "Awful Management" allows these malpractices to happen by sitting on their backsides, and not getting out there checking. A well-quoted phrase is, "You get what you pay for." My suggestion is check that you got what you ordered, and check that you got charged correctly.

Other costs

We said at the outset of this chapter that within most businesses and organizations the major areas of cost are employees, purchases, distribution, utilities, rent & rates, depreciation and finance costs. I have also said that in most manufacturing businesses the largest chunks of cost are within the people and purchasing costs, which we have just covered. The relative amounts spent on these elements of cost will vary from organization to organization. When looking at the finances of a business for the first time with a view to improvement, one should clearly look at the largest cost areas first. After looking at the Profit and Loss account for an overview, you should drill down to the next level within the Purchase and General Ledgers and ask if we need to keep buying this, and if we do, can we buy it any cheaper?

Unless you run your own fleet of transport, distribution costs can be treated as other purchased service. There are many excellent transport companies, so quality, price, delivery, and terms are the basis for a good "Dutch Auction" approach.

Transport is a fast changing and competitive market. It is appropriate that you challenge prices every six months. There are usually discounts for volume, and penalties for urgent deliveries. Your company's production and distribution departments need to be joined at the hip in order to hit dispatch dates and times, and so minimize distribution costs. On low profitability products, any potential profit can be lost by paying a special delivery rate because you are late. "Awful Management" has direct and indirect consequences.

Utilities cover the areas of gas, electricity and water. What you spend on utilities is determined by price per unit, and how many units you use. Again, there are opportunities for "Dutch Auctions" across all utility services providers. The opportunity for negotiation can happen annually with the gas and electricity providers. This is a fast moving market and prices have been changing rapidly. The volumes of gas, electricity, and water used relate directly to the processes and amenities provided in the business. There are many government-sponsored initiatives to help businesses cut usage. The most important thing you can do regarding utility costs is to make one person in the organization responsible for minimizing all utilities spend.

Rents are usually pre-determined at the start of a 5 or 10-year contract. For commercial properties they are significant costs. There is money to be saved by using a professional negotiator, who knows the local market. They usually offer a "no win - no fee" basis and twenty per cent charge for any savings they make. I cannot remember not winning on this basis.

Rates are worth investigating at least every two years in case you are paying too much. Here again, local specialists can help you negotiate down the amounts you pay. One of my mentors once said, "Everything in life is negotiable." I think he was nearly right. Everything should be challenged.

Depreciation is one for the accountants. Put simply, you spread the cost of major purchased items which are not for re-sale over a number of years. The number of years spread is agreed by the Finance Director and the external auditors. The more capital plant and development work you invest in, the greater the annual depreciation cost.

Other overheads like audit and legal services should be reviewed regularly to stop relationships becoming too cozy. Many companies stick with the same set of auditors, year in year out, on the basis that the auditors won't have to learn all about the business again. The Government is considering a compulsory change of auditors after a certain number of years.

Financing and Banking costs can be cash sponges. The people you are dealing with will be some of the cleverest and nicest people you will ever meet. So be careful. There is a correlation between intelligence and wealth.

The old adage is true. Banks like lending you money – particularly when you don't need it. From the bank's perspective, it is safer to lend money to those that can repay it. The bank starts from an absolutely clear position. It wants its money back, with interest. The time to negotiate with banks is when you are in a position of strength, such as at the outset of a project, when you have other banking options, or when you are well funded. Once you become weak, then you are weak indeed, and what was once your business can quickly become the bank's, in part, or in full!

Chapter 6 – "Awful Management" Checklist

1. Always employee friends and family - ahead of talent.
2. Don't define where employees fit into the organization.
3. Never let employees know what you require of them.
4. Match car parking spots with employee numbers.
5. Eliminate HR procedures, so that you can sack at will.
6. Ignore all subsequent solicitor correspondence.
7. Only buy from long established friends.
8. Never challenge any price or invoice – you might offend.
9. Leave lights and heating running on a night, to dissuade burglars
10. Never change auditors or banks. New people might be nosier.

QUALITY

Chapter 7 - QUALITY

Early exposure

Quality. What is it? What does it mean?

Back in the sixties, around September time, the "Marshall Ward" catalogue would arrive through the front door. It was over two hundred and fifty pages thick and filled with everything needed for the modern home. More importantly, it contained a section showing toys available for Christmas. I spent hours poring over the pictures and descriptions of the various games, toys and mechanisms.

I always wanted a "Dan Dare" radio station, with its two radio towers, microphones of the "pull hard on the string" type, sci-fi looking knobs, and bright red dials. Unfortunately, Dad's earnings didn't run to such extravagance. I never did get one as child. However, after a fifty-year wait, and thanks to e-bay and two sympathetic sons, I now have a second-hand set. Patience is a virtue.

After much deliberation over the catalogue contents, Mam would fill in the order form. This was placed, along with the appropriate postal order (cheques for the poor), into a stamped addressed envelope and posted off to the catalogue people. Some weeks later, and hopefully before Christmas, the goods would arrive. The "Spirit of Santa" would then hide them in the wardrobe, at the back of Mam and Dad's bedroom.

I only once looked in there before the great day - it ruined Christmas. I never did that again!

As a child, the last few weeks before Christmas seem to take forever. Eventually, the great day came and for the fifth year in a row the "Dan Dare" radio station did not materialize. There must be a war on Planet Pluton I thought, and their need for radio sets is clearly greater than mine. However, not a bad second best, - I had an electric car racing set. The early sets had rubber based tracks and metal cars. They were extremely expensive. During the sixties the use of plastics in toys became more and more prevalent, and the price of an electric car set came down. Below the price of a "Dan Dare" radio station.

I was now a proud car owner...

Amidst the torn Christmas wrapping paper, enough room was made to lay out this shiny, now plastic, replica of Silverstone. It was just shorter, by fourteen corners and a couple miles of tarmac. The red and blue cars were tentatively placed, their location pegs poking between the shiny contact guide rails. All of the electrical connections were checked, and then: 1...2...3...GO!

The red car shot off down the track, as if driven by some alcohol enthused youth the height of an acorn. Plastic boy totally ignores the first bend, driving straight on, straight off, hitting a box of dates before somersaulting and coming to a dead stop against the side of a selection box. The blue car had never moved - I was gutted!

"Awful Management" somewhere within the manufacturer's design, manufacturing, warehousing, dispatch, or quality functions had ruined my Christmas. The product had not come up to the expectations of its disappointed new owner. It had not worked right first time. Its six sigma was sick sigma. Where the hell was Dan Dare just when I needed him? Irrelevant question anyway. I hadn't got one of his radio sets - no means of contacting my Superhero. Unfortunately, I was too young for alcohol. But Mam did have some whisky filled chocolates on her pile - for a while.

Developing a quality product

A good place to start when setting out on the road to supplying good quality goods or services is to find out what the customer really wants. Practitioners of "Awful Management" will totally ignore the customer, and the market. Better to guess. We know best.

I said earlier, everything in life is a process. The achievement of excellent quality and reliability comes from establishing repeatable processes. The first step of this process is agreeing what the customer wants, setting the product or service specification.

It's not easy to get a bunch of customers, sales people, designers, engineers, purchasing people, production people, logistics people, and the quality team to finalize a specification. I'm sure you remember the phrase, "A camel is a horse designed by a committee." Developing specifications can be a nightmare, but it is absolutely essential that the specification be agreed before you start!

If you are developing a new mechanical part, then the main driver for the specification will be the required end function, sizes and fits. However, when you are agreeing the specification for something that allows much more artistic and creative freedom, then it can be a real nightmare to interpret what is in the other person's head, and to get it down on paper and signed off as part of the contract. Beauty is in the eye of the beholder. Sometimes you feel like you are in the famous artwork, "The Scream," but you still need an agreed specification before you start, and incur costs.

Once there is an agreed specification, signed by all parties, we are ready to start designing and drawing, thinking deeply and creatively. Highly charged creative people need a copious supply of coffee, bacon and egg sandwiches, prolonged lunch breaks, and cigarette breaks. "Awful Management" ignores this advice at its peril.

Good news - today smokers are sent, like convicts, to the outer reaches of the premises. Back in the eighties, our design offices were over seventy metres long and twenty-five metres wide. They were filled with both pipe and cigarette smoking draughtsmen. You could see nothing above waist height other than smoke, hanging like a November fog over the Manchester ship canal.

One of the great problems with designers is they are like hiccups. They don't know when to stop and they can't stop unless you give them a jolt or stop them breathing. Some years ago, I was taken on as the Interim CEO of an AIM listed company. A lot of money had been raised to develop clever electronic parts. There was a wide range of potential uses for worldwide markets. The upside could have been enormous. The problem was that the leader of the business just couldn't stop inventing. All the monies raised were getting burnt up, but no products were getting out into the market. The business had great ideas but it had no sales. Unsustainable!

Investing in product development has parallels with gambling on a horse race. If you bet on one horse, that one might not be the winner, so let's bet on two horses and increase our chances of winning. But that increases the cost of investment as well. You have to bet on every horse in the race to make sure you will back the winner and that is a very expensive way to play.

Investing in product development can be even worse than betting on a horse race - there is no guarantee that the product will work and that it will sell in the volumes and at the prices predicted.

To increase your chances of success, you have to prioritize. This should be based on the market probability of success, the technical probability of success, capital available for investment and potential returns. The entire senior team should collaborate to focus on only the top three projects. Many potential projects can be on the list, but the only work should be on the top three. Not until one of the top three is completely finished should work start on a new project.

We adopted this approach with our habitual invention team. Progress did improve, but not until we overcame the next issue - "time syrup". This is where time flows neither in straight lines, nor at a constant speed. It moves like thick syrup on an undulating surface, as observed by a drunk, with grease on his cracked glasses...

It was my first day with the HIT. There was a project meeting planned for 10.00 a.m. The allotted time came, and I sat there – alone. I sat musing, and waiting, with coffee cup in hand. The Project Manager finally turned up at 10.15 a.m. He'd just finished his cereals and was now ready to face the day, bless him! After a few grunts, he summoned the rest of his team. I introduced myself, the rest of the team did the same, and then I asked the Project Manager to take us through the Project Plan and the minutes of the last Project Meeting. There was a frightened look on his face. The others looked down at their shoes. I sensed the game was up?

Now Project Management infers the need for time management, progress against certain goals and targets, and some form of written record, or laptop to screen presentation. I'd already noticed that the Project Manager was wearing no watch. He had no project plan. He had no diary. He had turned up late. His team had turned up late. The company was burning money. Nothing was being achieved. This was how they managed and presented themselves. The combination of too many projects and poor project management was killing them. The start of the turnaround process was not too difficult. We focused on three projects. Watches, diaries, pads and pens were issued, along with words of encouragement!

Once our Design Team has a signed specification, they can start having fun developing designs and concepts on paper, CAD (computer aided design), laptops or PCs. The Team work diligently through well-described Design and Quality processes, recording thoughts and changes as they go, until they have a result. This can be solid "proof of concepts," "mock ups," "samples," or "trial parts," ready for testing and proving. This should be against an agreed time and cost plan. However, in product development...

You don't know what technical problems you may encounter!

You don't know what they will cost to overcome!

You don't know how long they will take to overcome!

There is always an element of the unknown with product development and feedback from customer trials.

After thousands of coffees, sausage sandwiches, trips to the perimeter, screams, shouts, the throwing of objects at the wall, the taking of pain killers, irate discussions with colleagues and the final sign-off of the new product, along with its supporting production and quality documentation - we are ready to make real ones! Crack open the diet coke and rip the top off that new tin of chocolate biscuits.

Producing a quality product

We need quality parts to make quality goods, so we need to start by looking at the quality of parts and products from our suppliers. The more critical the part, or the more money you are spending with a supplier, then the more time and effort you need to spend with them, establishing quality procedures to "Trust but audit" against later.

During one turnaround assignment, the key to the whole project was the development and launch of a newly patented high-tech product. There were issues during development with some of the electronics. An investigation showed the supplier had given us quality issues with similar electronics in the past. Our electronics engineer had not highlighted this to the Purchasing and Quality Teams, but we had a problem and we had to fix it...

We set off down the road on a six-hour journey to see the supplier, with an overnight stay. The accommodation and evening meal were excellent. The menu was clean and simple to understand and I got exactly what I had ordered. The menu on display at our table matched exactly what they were using in the kitchen. The kitchens were through the half windows and everything looked stainless steel shiny or dressed in clean bleached whites. The food tasted good and I slept well. Breakfast was equally good. I set off to meet the troublesome supplier powered by best bacon, eggs, tomatoes, toast, and spoilt with Earl Grey tea.

The Managing Director and Finance Director met us in their reception - a rather brown place. We were politely corralled into an equally brown boardroom. There we had with beverages, biscuits, and an update on the local football performance. To be fair, these were nice guys and they new their stuff.

Firstly, we checked if they had the correct drawing revisions. They hadn't, but they had been pleading for updates. In this "restaurant" the customer and kitchen menus were slightly different. We then had a walk around the factory. The housekeeping needed a bit of work – dust particles and electronic devices don't mix. We also agreed that we needed a common approach to testing components. The supplier and our engineers were using different tests - one tasted the food, the other sniffed it. This gave different perspectives and argument. The visit showed there had been "Awful Management" of supplier quality. By working with the supplier, things got better fast.

Once parts and goods arrive at your site, you can choose to inspect them or not. If you choose to inspect then you must determine what to inspect, pass and fail criteria, and what percentage of the delivery to inspect. The aim is to build up confidence that the supplier is achieving good quality at the factory so you have confidence in what is arriving at your factory. Then you can flex the level of Goods Inward Inspection accordingly.

This approach assures the quality of products and goods going into your assemblies and processes. The ultimate test is that supplied parts assemble easily and perform reliably in the customer's environment.

***

It's a common mistake to confuse Quality Control and Quality Assurance, although the clues are "Control," and "Assurance."

Quality Control encompasses checking, testing, sorting, and controlling product.

Quality Assurance embraces the writing of Quality Procedures, and the review of Quality Records, to assure oneself that the procedures and controls are effective.

In the world of "Awful Management" the Quality Department is just a pain in the backside – a cost centre full of softies that just keep stopping production. In truth, the Quality Department is an investment. It reduces waste, rejects, customer complaints, and it increases the quality of products perceived by the customer, leading to increased profits.

Keeping records and writing procedures may sound very, very, dull. It is this attention to detail that will lead to increases in productivity and bring down costs, as everything starts to become right first time. To keep it this way requires diligence, determination, and regular checking (auditing). To keep the quality systems fresh, alive, constantly improving, it is essential that independent audits be carried out. These should be at planned regular intervals. Remember, "Trust but audit!"

If you prefer an "Awful Management" approach, "Trust but don't audit."

Large chunks of my working life have been spent on productivity improvement, and quality improvement, across a wide spectrum of industries. At one end, the development and implementation of a Quality Assurance System for a seafood company processing langoustines, at the other end was steel machetes manufacture.

The former company is still in business. Its products frequent the chill cabinets of my local supermarket. The latter company eventually shut down after frequent break-ins, and the alleged use of its product in a high profile murder. But quality can be fun...

I was in Birmingham, auditing a customer's Quality Assurance System when struck by an unprofessional moment. The customer manufactured domestic heating and plumbing parts. The factory consisted of a large Victorian building, with a separate office block.

A former University colleague ran the business, a fellow metallurgist and, fortunately, a man with a good sense of humour.

It was a cold winter's morning as we slipped and slided across to the factory. As we walked, we chattered away about old times, and the boozy nights, down at the Union bar. We entered the factory and set off walking between the banks of old presses. They stood like metal soldiers: cold, dirty, greasy, and erect – thumping to their reggae beat.

After a long cold walk, we reached the Goods Inwards Department. My shoe polishing efforts of the previous evening were now completely wasted. Bill the Warehouse Man met us. A nice chap, and blessed with that fantastic West Midlands accent. We set about Quality Auditing the stores and its written procedures. There were no written procedures – "Awful Management".

Bill had worked there forever. "He knows what he's doing," said my University friend. I started to leaf through some "proof of delivery" paperwork. Written on one of these green pieces of paper was, "50 nuts." "Have you received these?" I enquired. "Oh yes," Bill replied confidently. "What kind of nuts are they?" I asked. Bill replied confidently, "Oh nuts that go into our Fabrication Department. They use them all the time." Aghast I continued, "But you use hundreds of different types, which are these?" Bill thought for a minute and then replied, like a man just given another job he could do without, "I dunno, but they've obviously taken them, and I'll have to bloody order some more!"

Air shot from my lungs, up through the giggle valve, and straight out through the laughter box. I could constrain myself no longer. With tears rolling down my cheeks, I attempted an apology. No good. My loud laughing continued. I gave it a minute - a bit better. I took a few deep breaths and was about to re-engage. But then the ever-cool Bill, with his lovely accent, said "'Yow orr right?" That immediately triggered me into another round of guffaws, outbursts and tears. I just managed to squeak an apology and took myself off back to the offices. I was quickly followed by my, now former, University mate who quite rightly exclaimed, "What the f***'s up with you?"

In short, there had been no written Quality Assurance procedures. The delivery note didn't say which parts had been ordered. There was no way Bill could check he'd got what he had ordered. Truly "Awful Management".

After a coffee and I'd calmed down, old friendships were re-established. I went back later that morning to apologize to Bill. During the next few months we all had a great time working on the implementation of a full Quality System. Soon after, when the guys got their well-earned accreditation, we were in a good part of the world for an excellent celebration - down the Curry House!

The Designers have done their stuff. The Suppliers have worked with us. The Quality Team has controlled and assured. We have good quality parts and products sitting on the warehouse shelves, ready to pass through the hole in the wall - to the wonderful world of production/manufacturing/assembly. However, caution! "Awful Management" rarely orders exactly the right number of parts. It orders too many or too few...

When it orders too many parts they will sit in the stores longer than planned. They will slowly start to rust, or deteriorate and at speeds that vary depending on the material, the packaging, the temperature, humidity, and the state of the warehouse, particularly its roof and resistance to rain penetration. It is essential that there are regular Quality Audits on the products and goods held within warehouses. Everything ages - sorry!

The guys and gals in the Production Department have now been given a Works Order, an internal document telling them what to make and how many. Production utopia is where everyone achieves the specified quality on a consistent basis. To achieve this level of production utopia it requires great attention to training, clear work and assembly instructions, tools and materials in the right places, all well stored and maintained, excellent housekeeping, clear and practical quality control procedures, high morale, and a great sense of urgency.

The goods have been designed. Purchasing, Stores, Production and Quality have done their jobs. The goods are ready for dispatch to the customer. We are almost there. The dispatch teams now throw the goods as far as they can into the back of the lorry or van. The goods rattle around during their one hundred and fifty mile journey to the docks. They are unloaded and sit out in the rain for four hours. The cardboard boxes get wet and weak.

Eventually the goods go into a container and are loaded onto a ship. They sit in their wet, weakened cardboard boxes. The rise and fall of the rolling ship has the effect of launching the goods through the weakened sides of the soggy cardboard. The structure and integrity of all the goods on that pallet is weakened. All of the cases burst. The goods are tossed around like pants in a washing machine.

I have known every element of this story to happen. It is "Awful Management" to give little time and attention to the areas of packaging and transportation. The product is finished the majority of the costs associated with it have been incurred. There is more money to be lost by not packaging and transporting the goods correctly than at any other point of the process. You would not spend all year raising a prize cow for market, and then drag it by one leg, on its side, through the mud to get there.

Quality Culture

I was lucky that my early career started within the Quality Departments of two FTSE 100 companies. The lucky bit is members of the Quality Department get to interface with every element of the business: Sales, Purchasing, Design, Manufacturing, Stores, Marketing, and even Finance. It's a great place to learn a lot about business, and one of its most common traits - resistance to change!

The theorists say things like change only happens when there is a need - such as a need to run to something or a need to run away from something. The "carrot or the stick" approach. "Awful Management" favours the stick approach - it doesn't need much thought, communication and time. The more intellectual approach to culture change is first sell the ideas and philosophy, through intellectual argument and discussion. Sometimes you need both...

We were making expensive high quality equipment, for power stations around the world. We had gone through the process of establishing good written procedures, lots of training, and lots of visits from the Electricity Board's Quality Auditors. They were absolutely red hot at what they did. The quality of what went out of the door was very good, it had to be, but we spent an awful lot of time and money getting it there. Costs mounted up, particularly on reworking parts that had failed on final electrical test.

For a couple of months, towards the end of a particularly large and late contract, we were getting a very high failure rate on electrical final inspection. This meant we weren't shipping and invoicing fast enough. That gets both good and "Awful

Management" annoyed. The Managing Director was definitely on my case and the number of bast***s had increased markedly.

High voltage testing was an expensive and time-consuming business. It involved large cranes, fitters, and testers, filling large vessels with expensive rare gas. Each test would take a day from start to finish.

We were talking thousands of pounds a go. We stood in the safety of the test office, looking out through the glass panels at the large assemblies of gas filled pressure vessels with ever increasing voltages tensing at their bodies and insulation. Simultaneously the tension within the assembled throng rose as we inched the voltage ever upwards – towards 750,000 volts!

Unfortunately, on too many occasions we would hear the heart wrenching sound of "CRACK." This meant turn everything off, de-gas, start again, and another "bullocking" and inquisition. We were running into time penalties. We had to carry on, but we had to improve matters in parallel. So we drove on, we converted the open assembly areas into clean room areas, we improved the working practices and things got a little bit better, but not enough, and then we found out why.

Historically the assembly inspection team had seen themselves closely aligned with production. Both the production and quality teams needed to progress work through the building to achieve the common aims – get it out, get it right. Unfortunately, the inspectors had got into the habit of letting un-inspected assemblies move to the next phase of assembly, on the basis that they would inspect for both the previous and additional assembly work at the same time. If the previous element were wrong, £10,000 of additional assembly work would be wasted. Bad decision – "Awful Management".

This was bad and in my department. I had already spoken to all of my inspectors about the need to hold production until it had been inspected and passed. They were not to cave in to production pressure. They were to let me know if overtime or extra resources were needed to keep both quality and production flowing.

My Inspectors had received written procedures. We had tried to sell the quality and need for cleanliness cultures to them! However, our investigations found the "final inspection team" was not always carrying out the prescribed cleaning and cleanliness checks within the pressure vessels, before taking them by crane to the electrical test facility. Fine particles and dust that should have been removed were causing the chambers to fail, as the high voltage electricity shorted to earth through these floating bodies. I was mad!

The assembly inspector involved happened to be a Shop Steward.

His disciplinary hearing, planned for 2.00 p.m., was the talk of the canteen. I could have sold tickets for the event. However, just like Sunderland beating Leeds in the Cup Final, the outcome was not what everyone expected…

We assembled in my office, a small greenhouse within the assembly cathedral. I kicked off, recalling the alleged events of recent days and asking why he had let things pass through without inspection. As predicted the answer was, "To help production." I then had to decide whether to sack him or discipline him. There had been no culture of discipline in the business up to this point. It would be ground breaking whichever way I bounced, and so I decided to give him an unheard of final warning! Upon hearing my decision the highly unionized Inspector leapt to his feet and screamed at me, "Right you BAST***, that's the last time I let anything through without inspection!" I replied, "That's just what I've been asking you to do all along. Thank you!" - and just then, the Final Whistle blew!

Chapter 7 – "Awful Management" Checklist

1. Have no specifications agreed with customers - keep it loose.
2. Have no Quality Procedures – keep it vague.
3. Have no time and respect for the Quality Department – a given.
4. Do not prioritize development projects.
5. Do not tightly project manage development projects.
6. Do not allow customers to trial new products before release.
7. Always source supplies from your friends – accept anything.
8. Have a "Do what the Hell you like culture" - control is creepy.

LOOK AFTER THE CASH

Chapter 8 - LOOK AFTER THE CASH

What the Dickens

Charles was right. If you consistently spend more than you earn – look out, big trouble ahead!

One of "Awful Management's" traits is to continue spending more than the organization brings in, then shout foul when they go bust and close. If we are talking about one self-employed person, then tough! But if the organization employs tens, hundreds, or thousands of people, then that is a disaster. Everyone can end up out of a job. I have seen too many grown men and women crying in the office because "Awful Management" has led to painful changes. Despite the fact that the employees have given their all, they are out. The employee then has to go home to the heartache of telling the family the bad news. More tears come, and then the hard realities of life without work and with little income. Living standards take a dive. Self esteem and dreams fade into emptiness. Self-doubt increases and relentless self-questioning debilitates and tires.

A much better scenario is to have a growing profitable business, well funded, paying its bills on time, with excellent financial systems and reports in place to ensure adequate planning and provision for the sunshine days and the rainy ones. Even in such a well run business the occasional administrative error can lead to unwanted excitement...

I had just joined a major quoted plc company and it was my first hour in the role as Divisional Managing Director. The business had a turnover of £50M per annum and it was very profitable. I had just seen my office. It had oak-panelling, a large oak board table, twelve leather covered chairs, and at the head of the table a Managing Director's throne.

The tea had arrived with mandatory chocolate biscuits. I was about to meet my new team. My secretary rushed in to the office, her face long drawn and troubled. Leaning over the throne she whispered, "There's a bailiff in reception and he wants to see you!"

My first thought was, "What the hell have I got into here?" My second thought was, "I'd better go down to reception straight away, and see if I need to start looking for a new job tomorrow." Now bailiffs come in many interesting forms. This gentleman was just that, a gentleman. After the usual pleasantries, it transpired our highly profitable, multi-national plc owed his client £56, plus costs. There had been some oversight in our administrative system and we had never seen the bill. After investing some of the tea and biscuits in the gentlemen, and giving him a cheque for the appropriate amount, we cordially parted company. Looking back it was no big deal, but at the time it was frightening and horrible.

On another occasion, in another company, the lovely lady in reception phoned my office. Whispering into the phone she said, "There are half a dozen big blokes in reception demanding money. You'd better come straight away!" Now having met a bailiff once before, I thought I was thoroughly trained in the art of dealing with the profession. I wasn't!

In reception stood six very large gentlemen. They looked like tough pirates, with tattoos everywhere and few teeth. They were not people to mess with. Their Captain opened with, "Your Company owes money. We have come to take away all of your machines. We have a low loader outside for them!" Not bad for starters, I thought. I replied, "If there are no other options I will get my lads to help. But first, can we have a cup of tea and see what we can sort out?"

It turned out the Finance Director had not paid an old bill on the date he had agreed. The supplier had had enough and sent the bailiffs in.

Eventually the tea, biscuits, and cheques for the creditor, the Captain, the Pirates, and the good ship "Low-loader" did the trick - but again, not a very nice experience. You feel very threatened, and not in control when pirates attack you.

The root cause of our tight cash-flow problems in this company was our fast rate of growth. We needed additional working capital but the Finance Director was not moving fast enough. After the pirate caper we had the FD walk the plank – there are no College lectures on this stuff!

Financial problems escalate further when the bank loses its confidence in "Awful Management's" ability to pay bills on time. The bank may throw out "Awful Management" and appoint its own Administrators to run the business as a going concern. The business may yet be saved, so the bank gets its money out, and many jobs may be saved. Administrators are highly trained and with loads of experience. Fortunately, the only time I ever came into contact with an administrator on a professional basis, was to deprive him of a job...

The bank was only weeks away from appointing an administrator at a friend's failing engineering business. In a state of panic, the Managing Director of this business phoned me to see if we could keep the Administrator out and save the business. I said I'd be with him in the morning and got the car loaded up for another early morning start. The crux of the problem was too much labour, and not enough work. The jobs to be made redundant were filled by long-term employees and the business had no money for expensive redundancies.

Working with the Management Team and the unions, we agreed a plan whereby the long-term employees would be re-trained, so allowing shorter-term employees to be released. These cheaper redundancies were affordable. The business continued and ninety jobs were saved. Two weeks later, we put the plan before the bank.

A potential administrator sat at the table with the bankers. He looked at my client as a crow looks at a breakfast of road killed rabbit. Having listened to our plans the bank team turned to the potential Administrator and asked, "Do you think the plan will work?" The gentleman (not a crow at all) replied, "Yes, I really think that is the right approach!" So that is exactly what we did, saving business and jobs. The business is still running years later. It now has exciting product ranges and new routes to market.

You don't want to get that close to closure!

Where the bank does not believe the business has any chance whatsoever of continuing as a going concern, they appoint a Receiver. That job is simply to turn as much of what is left of the business into cash. The cash pays back the Bank's loans and creditors. Thankfully, I have no anecdotes about Receivers!

Profit is Queen but "Cash is King"

Businesses can make profits but go bust. How does that work?

Imagine you are selling wonder-bars. You pay £100 for each one and sell them for £120. That is £20 profit for every wonder-bar that you sell. Marvellous business!

However, the supplier needs paying when you collect the wonder-bars. The customers are all outside the UK and they pay you six months after each delivery. Cash is King, because you need to get the money back from the customers to re-invest in new stocks of wonder-bars.

You could accelerate the process by investing more of your own money in the business. Then the more wonder-bars you buy, the more you can sell and the more profit you can make. You could accelerate even faster by borrowing money from a bank, venture capitalist, or private equity house. It sounds simple and so you do it...

Then some customers say that they want a range of wonder-bars.

The supplier agrees to supply you, but he wants an order showing how many of each type. He still wants you to pay him up front. In the absence of a written order from your customers, you have to forecast (a professional word for guess) what quantities and types of wonder-bars your customers will take each week. Guesses are not firm orders, so you have a stock of slow selling wonder-bars to fund, as well as your ongoing weekly purchases of wonder-bars. It gets worse...

Some customers are having a tough time selling the products and cannot pay you on time. They need another couple of months.

You need to find new customers. The sales team get a bonus for increasing volume. The new customers have no experience of selling the product, so they accept the sales team's offer of the goods on sale or return. That means the customer doesn't have to pay until they have made a sale themselves. It may be a very long time before you get the money. You now need money for your own stock and stock held by your customers. At the same time, the flow of money back into the business is slower and less predictable.

To support your rapidly growing wonder-bar business you have taken on new large premises, more staff, bigger loans, and office equipment with high monthly rentals. But hey! Good News! Your sales invoices exceed the purchase costs for those items sold. On paper, you are making a profit. Then your telephone rings. The lady at reception whispers into her phone, "There are six large gentlemen in reception!"

Although you have more customers every week, you have more bills than you can pay with the cash available - due to "Awful Management". Profit is Queen but Cash is King!

The key role of the Finance Director is to make sure that you don't run out of cash. It is even better if you don't run out of cash and have money to invest in the growth of the business. "Awful Management" does not secure enough cash to run the business and does not look after the assets it has. To stay on top of cash management the five primary tools for a good Finance Director are:

Standard Cost analysis to find the costs of production and delivery.
Profit and Loss account showing Sales - Costs = Profit.

Balance Sheet to show Net Assets and Capital Employed.
Source & Application to show Funds in and out.
Cash flow forecasts to show expected funds in and out.

Whenever you start looking at an organization, these are the key reports to look at. Their quality, content, and availability will quickly tell a trained eye the state of the nation. In the world of "Awful Management", we have already seen that some of these vital reports may not be available. They may be incomplete, and are probably out of date or inaccurate. Therefore, "trust but audit".

Sources of cash

A brand new business needs new money. The obvious sources are you, friends and family, moneylenders, banks, venture capitalists, private equity houses, wealthy individuals, business angels, government agencies, and there are other options on the internet – with and without "health warnings"!

The very last time I saw Granddad Sheard, you may remember the miner turned fish and chip shop owner turned turf accountant, he sat in his chair next to the window. At the time, I was working as a Management Consultant in one of the world's premier Venture Capital houses. Granddad knew this and was always up for a bit of bear baiting.

Granddad turned slowly in his chair, and looking straight at me through his twinkling mischievous eyes, enquired, "Have you borrowed money to buy your new house?" "Yes Granddad," I replied, waiting for the well prepared follow on. "I'd rather eat from dustbins than borrow off those bast*** banks," he snapped. "Why's that Granddad?" I asked, already knowing the answer, after years of coaching from this Yorkshire thoroughbred. "Well, they lend you the money. Then they want it back, plus interest – and if you don't pay it back on time, they take your house away from you!" This was followed up with another Bast***s!" Awful language.

A fundamental of being lent money is that you can show the potential lender you have the ability to pay it back. Today there is a standard approach adopted by most lenders. This starts with the potential borrower having a good business story, supported by a good business plan. The plan should show the intended market place, product or service offering, projected sales and costs, cash generation and flows, and projected profits over the next 3-5 years. It also helps if you then have an excellent presentation and presenter. It pays to shop around, because just like on "The Dragons' Den" the deal may also cost you a shareholding in addition to loan and interest repayments.

Friends may be a potential source of funding. However, they will only remain friends if all repayments are met as promised. When Granddad Sheard came out of the mining industry, injured after the coal seam roof collapsed and broke his hip, Granddad needed money. At that time, Granny had a very good friend who was married to a man in the circus. Honestly, I'm not making this stuff up. Now we've all seen those circus images of the man with his tights pulled up his bottom and the straps over the shoulders, like some medieval torture. The man carries one of those large barbells, with metal spheres at either end- the classic image of the strong man in the circus.

Granny's best friend's husband was that man in the circus!

Granddad's new life-style, out of the pit, was founded on a loan from the strongman in the circus. The money borrowed was invested first in one fish and chip shop, and then a second, before the whole lot was sold and the money used to invest in a village turf accountancy practice. That is posh for "bookie". My childhood was during the "bookie" period. Mid-week for me was life on the council estate, but weekends were spent in relative luxury out motor cruising on Granddad's riverboat. The loan from a friend had worked out. During the winter sometimes, Gran and Granddad would take me to visit their old friends at the coast where they had retired. They were a lovely old couple. But would you have borrowed money from a circus strongman?

There are plenty of sources to raise money for funding. As I have said previously, you need a good story and a good business plan to get you underway. The same is true for an existing business that needs to raise money for growth, or a new project with long-term potential. If you have a good story, or you are doing well and don't need additional money (irony), you can raise new finance. However, in the world of "Awful Management" you will either be not making money or you will have run out of it. Neither the man at the bank nor the circus will lend you anymore. You have to generate some cash within your business.

The main options to generate cash within the business are:

Increase the profits by increasing sales prices & reducing costs.
Reduce the stock by holding less of everything.
Pay slower, for example by pay in 60 days rather than 30 days.
Get paid quicker, for example being paid in 30 days rather than 60 .
Sell assets, for example divisions/land/buildings/equipment/stock.

When "Awful Management" is running out of money, action needs to be immediate. You may not have long before those six rough types are standing in your reception demanding chocolate fingers with menaces. Some of the ways to generate cash can take longer to be effective than others, but they need to be initiated in parallel...

Increase the profits

The quickest way to increase profits is to put your sales prices up. Ideally, you should base sales pricing decisions on accurate up-to-date standard costs and good information on competitor sales prices. In the absence of such information, you can only put up your sales prices based on an assessment of risk. That is not an ideal approach. For the top volume items, you need accurate standard costings to be available to you in hours - not days.

We covered in an earlier chapter the opportunity to increase profits through the negotiation of lower purchase prices, reducing the number of employees, and reducing other bills through negotiation. In times of crisis all of these areas have to be re-challenged, aggressively, and quickly to reduce the probability of meeting pirates in reception.

Reduce the stock

One of my old mentors used to walk me around the warehouse, run his fingers across the tops of the dusty boxes and say, "There Son, I don't need a computer to tell me what isn't selling!"

Some stock can just sit there forever and ever, Amen. Everyone walks past it day after day. After a time you don't notice the old stock anymore. It becomes part of the building, a historic relic, homage to previous Sales Directors and Stock Controllers of yester-year! Homage to "Awful Management"!

The stock was paid for with cash. It is there to be turned back into cash.

If you are running out of cash, go through the old slow moving stock. Can it be sold another way, such as on line, offered at rock bottom price, or moved through bottom feeders in the retail market. It needs to be turned into cash quickly.

The less you buy from your suppliers the less cash will be going out, so buy smaller quantities at a time. It may cost you slightly more for the privilege but you don't have to tie up your scarce money in stock. Ideally, you buy the goods and sell them straight away.

Good stock management is a major weapon in the armoury of good cash management. Bad stock management is a nasty virus that grows under "Awful Management" conditions. It wastes money, time and effort.

The key elements to a good stock management programme are a good sales forecast, the setting and re-setting of minimum and maximum stock levels on a regular basis, and tight stock control. Count them all in and count them all out again.

When the only stock on the shelves sells quickly, you are optimizing your investment in stock. You are also making sure that when a part or product is needed you can give good service. In too many stores, anyone can walk in and take out parts, without ever up-dating the paperwork or computer system. This tends to happen more on a nightshift, where stores are less likely to be manned. The production team need a part, they take it, they don't book it out, so the system thinks it has one more than it actually has. Some day a stores person will go looking for something that isn't there, and the customer will be let down. Open stores are excellent examples of "Awful Management"!

Stores need tight controls of what goes in and out, and who goes in and out, so the records always have up-to-the-second accurate data. When cash is tight we need to sell as much of the existing stock as quickly as we can. We need to sell at the best price we can get. We should only buy replacement stock that will sell quickly. At times of cash crisis the Finance Director will need to sign all Purchase Orders or Contracts that commit the organization to spending. In large organizations it will be necessary for the Finance Director to delegate lower levels of spend through a formal Signature Authorities Procedure.

Pay slower
When a business is really on the edge of the abyss, payments to anyone needs total control at the highest level in the organization. A classic Turnaround Manager approach is to get hold of all cheque books immediately, and gain control of all electronic methods of payment. It would be "Awful Management" to allow uncontrolled payments to be made when cash is so tight and critical to the day-by-day recovery.

Not paying is a very effective way of not spending. Unfortunately it can only be a very short-term measure. Payments will have to be made eventually, and will need prioritizing. One of the duties of a Company Director is to ensure that creditors are paid when their invoices become due for payment.

Knowingly increasing debts without the ability to pay can leave the Directors personally liable for the debts. You really don't want to lose the umbrella of protection that limited company status affords you as Director. To lose your house and possessions because some Purchasing Clerk ordered another £500,000 of widgets would be truly "Awful Management".

Through negotiation, you may agree with your suppliers and creditors to pay them more slowly. A programme of visits and presentations should be quickly undertaken to see suppliers, the bank, investors, HM Revenue & Customs, other creditors. In every case, you need a good story and a good recovery plan. The whole argument in persuading people to give you more time to pay depends on them believing that there is more chance of getting their money back by supporting the business than by pulling the plug now.

The first test of insolvency is whether you can pay your debts when they fall due. You are allowed to carry on trading, even if some of your bills are overdue, so long as the Board agrees that it is in the best interests of the creditors to continue trading. There must be a plan in place which the Directors all believe will get the creditors their money back. If one Director doesn't believe it, then that Director should resign, otherwise he may have personal liabilities to pay later should the recovery plan fail. All exciting, dangerous, nervous stuff caused in the first place by "Awful Management."

Get paid quicker

You may remember the, "Dear does not pay his bills" story. When I spoke to him, he paid and he came back for more! When you need money right now, get on those phones and chase. The first stop is to look at the Sales Ledger and see who owes you money beyond the period agreed. The late payer, the bast***s that owe you real money that can keep the business afloat! For the really old, stubborn late payers, send the Sales Representative around to collect a cheque.

If the honest direct approach doesn't work, then go down the legal route. The lawyers will try to reclaim your debt through the small claims court. Then they will hire your favourite professional chocolate finger eaters to go and collect monies owed to you!

Another route for accelerating cash generation is to offer your good payers an early settlement discount. The benefit is simple. By paying you back earlier than normal, the customers will receive a higher return than bank interest rate. If you have cash rich customers, this can be an attractive option and it can get you out of an immediate fix. Longer term, if you leave the early settlement discount on offer, it will cost you profit. Nevertheless, when cash is tight, offering early settlement discounts can allow you to live to play another day.

Sell assets - divisions/land/buildings/equipment/stock

Assets that no longer add value to the organization are called "lazy assets". They are not lazy "good for nothings". They may be good for cash! It is far better to sell something that you no longer need and generate cash from it than go bust. However, the bigger the item the bigger the emotional attachment can be.

When selling a division, you are selling a business. Like any other business sale, you need to engage professionals. They will put the best story together as to why the business is being sold, pull all of the numbers together, talk to management and create the "dream forecast," before marketing the business to both the trade and the investment houses. You want the professionals to run an auction process and maximize the sales price. This all takes time.

There is also a need to engage with professionals when selling land and buildings to maximize the possible returns. Now to this point, all my comments on generating cash relate to my experiences in the UK. I also used the same tried and tested approaches when working in Germany and the Czech Republic. The selling of property and land again raises the issue of culture. The way we view land and property can vary significantly with culture.

It was a hot, humid evening in Southern Germany. My German team of Directors and I were sitting upstairs in the dining room of a beautiful traditional Guest House. The windows were open. The flowers were in bloom in the pretty window boxes. Smells of excellent German cooking filled the room, and throughout the dining room good-humoured chatter abounded at every table, except ours!

The business was doing OK, and it was about to do even better on the back of some great new products that were coming to market. I wanted to raise additional cash to accelerate product development. Cash was fairly tight, and we could always do with some more cash to accelerate investment. A few weeks earlier, I had suggested that we sell one of our spare pieces of land located just outside the village, with the building that sat idly upon it. At first, my German colleagues had said that, "We will look into it."

Some weeks had now passed, so I enquired in my best German, "Where are we up to in finding a buyer for the land and building?" There were no answers, just three faces staring at their feet.

I repeated the question, "Where are we up to in looking for a buyer for the land and building?" Again no answer. By this point I was getting pretty fed-up with the three of them. Then the oldest broke ranks and said, "Gary we cannot do this, we will lose face in the community!"

After a few more large beers and some excellent food, we eventually got to the heart of the matter. In Germany, both land and buildings are highly prized. In these local farming communities, the land and buildings are passed on from generation to generation. It is very rare for such things to be sold, and usually only when a family has big financial problems. The selling of the company's land and buildings would cause a considerable loss of face for the Directors and everyone who worked in the company. They would only sell if there was absolutely no other option.

During the next few weeks, by some sort of miracle, the German Directors found the additional cash flow to accelerate product development. Sales prices were increased without me asking, and various slow moving stocks sold. With my aims achieved, we decided as a Board to keep the land and building, but with my caveat, "For now."

Once a year I order a skip from our local scrap dealer, in order to take away the junk, and anything we longer needed, in order to clear a pathway through my garage. The scrap dealers have probably changed their job title now to something like materials recycling engineers or savers of the environment. When I was a young lad, the rag and bone man came around the streets with his horse and cart, in "Steptoe and Son" fashion. He paid you for your scrap and old rags. He only paid you pennies, or gave you a balloon on a stick, but the horse sometimes left a bonus for the roses.

Just like most households, organizations accumulate "stuff". It can manifest itself in many ways. Let's take a virtual walk into a manufacturing business. You enter through the front door. There are paintings and perhaps sculptures. There are a couple of empty desks and chairs opposite the receptionist. You go upstairs to the Board Room to meet the team. More artwork on the walls, a spare projector in the corner, and as you are passed a cup of tea, you look out at the car park and you comment, "Those are very nice cars, are they company cars? Do we own them?"

After a cup of tea and introductory chat, you are taken for a walk around the factory. You pass machines that are not running. You run your fingers (in well trained, dust gathering fashion) across the top of the machines and ask, "When did this last run? When is it planned to run again?" You continue on your journey around the factory looking at everything that doesn't move, seeing pound signs. The Production Director declares that that is the end of the tour and you enquire politely, "Is it OK to go and have a look at the back of the factory?" Horror grips his entire body at this heart-piercing request. "Awful Management" never looks outside and definitely not around the back.

We press on, through the fire door, past the huddled smokers with their backs to the weather, and gaze upon three containers. No one has the key to these containers. It is believed that long ago, when they moved factories, some of the old machinery was put into these containers, just in case we ever needed them in the future. "Awful Management" doesn't know that the three containers are there, or know what is in them.

The Production Director reluctantly agrees to get the keys sorted. We move back into the factory. The smokers have now disappeared. We pass offices with empty desks and chairs, work benches with tools untouched, photocopiers and faxes of yester-year, cupboards with more stationery than a stationers in Stationery Street. Everywhere, there is cash tied up doing nothing. It all needs liberating, quickly.

We have already discussed the need to sell off slow moving and excess stock, and how to avoid getting back into an overstocked position. The combined efforts of selling and reducing these lazy assets will help the business to focus and improve morale. The very act of shifting out dust covered stock and equipment will show positive change as well as generating additional cash for the business. "Awful Management" had been wasting this lifeblood!

Business Turnarounds

The two main reasons that businesses get into trouble are:

> *Awful Management, as described in this book*
> *Dramatic market change, like slide rules killed by calculators*

There is an argument that the makers of slide rules should have seen pocket calculators coming. They could have had new products in development to sustain the business through a dramatic change in the market place. They could have diversified. We can argue that there is only one real reason why businesses get into trouble: "Awful Management"!

Eventually with an under-performing business, the bank and shareholders will be pushing to make a change at the top of the organization. The "Awful Management Leader" will be removed and a

Turnaround Manager appointed. Ideally, the Turnaround Manager will be someone with considerable experience in that industry or sector, and with previous turnaround success.

The key elements of a successful turnaround strategy are well documented and are listed below. Note that many of the elements are simply best practice. They apply equally to the running of a good business and one in need of turnaround due to the earlier failings of "Awful Management".

Key elements of a successful turnaround strategy

Although no turnaround is the same, the strategy usually consists of:
. *Change of management*
. *Strong central financial control*
. *Product-market reorientation*
. *Cost reduction*
. *Asset reduction*
. *Organizational change*
. *Improved marketing*
. *Growth via acquisitions*
. *Investment*
. *Debt & Finance restructuring*
. *Keep key stakeholders informed*

Change of Management

In the majority of turnarounds, a new Chief Executive Officer is required in order to change the culture of the business. The removal of the previous CEO and the appointment of a Turnaround Manager signals to the investors, the bank, and all employees that things have to change and that the process has started.

Strong central financial control

The Turnaround Manager, working closely with the incumbent Finance Director, will take control over cheque books, electronic payment methods, purchase orders, and any potential contracts which commit the business to spend money. If a signature authority procedure does not exist, it is a priority to formulate and issue one. The rules must be communicated to everyone with authority to spend the company's money. If the procedures do exist, then they should be reviewed and updated on day one of the new regime. In the early days of a turnaround, the more control at the top of the organization the better.

Product-market reorientation

We need to understand very quickly where are we making profits and losses. There is an urgent need to have all product standard costs up-to-date so we can decide which products to promote, which prices to increase, and stop making any products where we still won't make a profit after improvements.

Cost reduction

We have already seen that everything in life is negotiable. We need to get on and achieve cost savings in every area of the business straight away. The key is to prioritize on the big spend areas first. Two hours spent on saving fifty quid a year on toilet roll expenditure could be better spent trying to save 5% off the £4M raw materials supply contract.

Asset reduction

Go and walk the place, ask the questions, look at the asset registers, and start selling those lazy assets to convert them into cash. Sell the slow moving stock at the best price you can get. Start reducing the levels of stock in the warehouses and out on the shop floor to reduce purchase spend and free up cash.

Organizational change

With Turnaround Management, change has to happen quickly. Judgment calls about the organization and individuals can take place on a day-by-day basis. It is not until the "Business Recovery Plan" has been formulated that the organizational structure, and the number of employees needed to deliver it, can be set up and implemented. The timing of this will depend on the size of the business and the size of the problems faced. Aim to look under all of the stones during the first month of the assignment, and start pulling the Business Recovery Plan together during the second month. The target is to have a Business Recovery Plan agreed by management, investors, and the bank within three months.

Improved marketing

Not until we are clear about what we want to sell, based on the standard costing exercise, do we want to unleash the marketers and the sales team, with the associated costs. Armed with good standard costs, competitive pricing information, and marketing and sales collateral we can go out and sell like hell.

Growth via acquisitions

A key piece of the preparatory work when compiling the Business Recovery Plan is a review of the market and competitors. This may reveal that a competitor is also struggling with the market conditions. If the acquisition of the competitor will increase combined profitability, through the reduction of combined overhead costs/site costs/better market pricing and perhaps generate some cash through the release of assets, then it may make sense to go into acquisition mode.

Investment in product development and capital equipment

Businesses in turnaround are characteristically short of money. They have limited ability to invest in product development or new equipment. Once liquidity improves, through any combination of strategies, then investment in areas that will support future sales growth/cost reduction can be considered.

A turnaround strategy based on product development can be risky. Product Development gives no guarantee of returns, and targeted completion dates will probably slip. If the core business was originally based on products and markets that were in decline, it may be the only choice for future growth!

Capital investment for productivity gains within operations or the office can reduce costs, improve competitiveness, and increase profits. While cash is in short supply it is essential that capital investments be prioritized in terms of affordability and quick return.

Debt & Finance restructuring

A business that finds itself in need of a turnaround is typically not generating enough cash to pay its creditors or the bank on time. Cash-flow generation strategies, particularly asset reduction, are most commonly used to reduce borrowings. There are two other financial strategies commonly used: debt restructuring, and raising additional finance. A combination of all three strategies may be necessary to give both sufficient liquidity and time for the completion of a turnaround.

We have already looked at improving liquidity through an asset reduction strategy, with examples such as the selling of divisions/ buildings/equipment/stock. We will now look at debt restructuring and the raising of additional finance.

Debt restructuring involves discussions with the bank. Typically the focus is on reducing the monthly repayment figure, but increasing the repayment period at a higher interest rate. The Bank may convert short-term debt into long-term debt, or convert some of its debt into various forms of share holding. There are many options, and you will invariably need the support of external advisors to get the best deal at a time of relative weakness. You may also get a sizeable bill from the bank for arranging all of this, plus their legal fees on top of your own advisor's fees. The good news is that you can pay the bank back its fees slowly, and your business lives another day!

The bank will rarely put additional finance into a business that is in need of a turnaround. It would be seen as "good money after bad". It can be a condition of the bank's financial restructuring that the shareholders have to waive some of their fiscal privileges, and put in additional funding. The Directors always have the option of moving to another bank. Once "Awful Management" has run the business to a point where a turnaround is necessary, it would be a brave bank that jumped into that breach!

Reducing assets is within the control of the Turnaround Team. Dealing with the shareholders, the banks and stakeholders will always need a very good story, a very good business-plan, very good numbers, all very well presented by credible management.

Keep key stakeholders informed

The appointment of a Turnaround Manager signals, "Attack Awful Management" to all stakeholders. From that point on, every stakeholder will want to know what is happening, what will happen next, and how will it affect me? The Turnaround Manager's Recovery Plan is based on the *"Key elements of a successful turnaround strategy"* laid out in this chapter. The approach needs communicating to the key stakeholders on day one of the turnaround. It is vital that the bank, shareholders and employees are updated regularly. They are all important!

Chapter 8 – "Awful Management" Checklist

1. Always spend more than you earn.
2. Let the Team decide how much to spend and on what.
3. Do no cash flow forecasting – these are just depressing guesses.
4. Ensure the warehouse is always full of stuff.
5. Pay suppliers quickly. They are your friends.
6. Don't chase customers for payment. They are your friends.
7. Invest in shiny equipment.
8. Invest in vague creative product development.
9. Keep bad news to yourself.
10. Hide excesses in containers at the back of the building.
11. Absolutely resist the appointment of a Turnaround Manager. They could be the death of you!

A SENSE OF URGENCY

Chapter 9 - A SENSE OF URGENCY

Imagine "Awful Management" applied to a Formula 1 racing team!

It's Monaco, and the drivers have been out testing their cars, gliding them along the smooth tarmac of the tightly winding compact streets. Stands, pavements, balconies, and boats are full to bursting with excited fans. They cheer and wave as the cars flick past. The hot Mediterranean sun is gently roasting the skins of the highly charged masses. Sunglasses, hats and team colours are the order of the day.

After the allotted half-hour of morning testing, the cars wind their way back into the pits. There they sit, receiving final checks before the 3.00 p.m. start. The crowds tuck into their lunchtime treats. The Glitterati promenade or display themselves from their yachts, resting on the silvery waters of the packed harbour. Many of the "yacht-less" are perched on the side of the hill, which overlooks this exotic mix of wealth, engineering, danger, gastronomy, gambling, intoxication, and a good day out!

At 3.00 p.m. the checkered-flag goes down. The 32 cars scream away from the start line, bursting the eardrums of any fool standing within 30 metres without ear-protection. Around the first corner, their high-pitched screams can be heard moving up and through the streets, as the cars approach the famous Monte-Carlo Casino. The race goes on...

Meanwhile, down in the pits, and in the back of the AMF1's garage, a card game has broken out, involving all of the AMF1 pit crew. This is Monaco, a gambling centre, after all!

Outside, the cars scream their high-pitched songs, the highly charged crowd buzzes, and the fumes coming from the cars smell like the finest brandy served in a rubber cups. Forty minutes into the race and some of the AMF1 pit crew are financially much better off as the card game progresses. Then, just as the next hand of cards is dealt, one of the AMF1 cars turns off the track and heads down the pit lane.

In the back of the AMF1 garage, the screaming and whining of the high-pitched engine cuts across the Lead Mechanic's call, "And I'll raise you fifty."

The AMF1 pit crew are more than a bit "p***ed off" by the noise coming from outside their garage door. The door was already slammed shut because of the cars ruining the card game. The Lead Mechanic eventually shouts at one of his juniors, "Bill, go see which one of those f*****g morons is revving his engine up, and ruining the game." Bill, reluctantly, goes out to see what all the fuss is about.

Sitting outside in his beautiful bright shiny AMF1 car is Giorgio.

When Giorgio drove for the people with the red cars, a pit stop was normally 8 seconds. He had been waiting outside the AMF1 garage for just under a minute. As Bill emerges from behind the garage door, Giorgio lifts his visor and shouts at Bill, "I need new tyres!" Bill replies, "Why?" Exasperated, Giorgio responds, "Look, I'm skidding all over the place and I need new tyres!" Bill slowly gets the message and toddles off back inside, leaving Giorgio alone in his car, to get more and more frustrated.

"Giorgio wants some new tyres," announces Bill, to his fellow card players. "How many does he want?" asks the Lead Mechanic. "I'll go back and ask him," responds Bill politely. "Giorgio, how many tyres do you want?" shouts Bill. "F*****g four!" screams Giorgio. Again, Bill toddles off back inside. Whilst outside, Giorgio is getting madder and hotter. Most competitors are screaming down the racing circuit. Other cars are being serviced in 8 seconds, right in front of Giorgio, as he looks on longingly.

Bill announces, "Giorgio wants four tyres," and asks, "Have we got any?" One of the pit crew stands up and replies, "I'll go and have a look, I think I ordered some." The clock ticks, and the cars and the seconds go by. The Lead Mechanic now throws his losing hand onto the table and snarls, "Come on lads, here are the 4 tyres that Giorgio wants, we'd better pack in the game, for now, and get them fitted." The pit crew throw down their cards, and saunter begrudgingly out to the pit lane – rolling the four tyres in front of them.

During the ensuing verbal fight between Giorgio and the Lead Mechanic, some of the pit crew carry on jacking-up the car. Then one of them starts to look for a wheel nut remover. He knows that they have one, because as he saw it this morning, during the practice session. Eventually he finds it, takes off one of the old tyres and fits a new one. The wheel nut remover is then passed to his mate on the adjacent wheel. Slowly, but surely the four tyres are replaced and Giorgio has a new set of tyres.

Flushed with success, the pit crew re-huddles, and turns from the car, setting off back to their card game. The last of the crew is just about to close the garage door when there is a loud yell from Giorgio, "Hey you bast***s, I want some fuel as well!"

The pit crew is now more than "cheesed off" at Giorgio's further interruption of their card playing. However, in a desperate bid to show leadership and "sense of Team" the Lead Mechanic shouts, "Come on then lads, let's show this loser what the AMF1 Team can do when it has to pull out all of the stops!"

One of the pit crew pulls the fuel delivery system towards the car, in readiness to slake the thirst of Giorgio's ever whining engine. The car's fuel cap is lifted, the fuel nozzle is pushed firmly into the fuel tank, and the "activate mechanism" is pressed firmly home. The other cars continue to scream past. The sun beats down, the clock ticks – BUT is the fuel flowing into Giorgio's petrol tank?

No- nothing!

"What the f***'s up with this thing, no fuel is coming out?" bellows the Fuel Man. A real fight now breaks out between Giorgio and the Lead Mechanic. Still sitting in the car, Giorgio has managed to get a hold of the Lead Mechanics head, and has him in a headlock. The Lead Mechanic now has his legs in the air, as Giorgio has pulled him across the cockpit. Meanwhile, one of the pit crew members is looking at the storage tank fuel gauge. It reads empty. "Empty," shouts the entire pit crew! Bill chips in, "Oh, I know why that is. The fuel company wouldn't deliver any more because we never pay our bills!"

Just then the second AMF1 car rolls into and along the pit lane. It has been out on the track for too long, and has now run out of petrol. It rolls the last fifty metres to an embarrassing stop.

Both AMF1 cars are now dead. They have no fuel. They have no money to buy fuel, tyres, or wages. There is no money to pay the Bank or Investors. Team AMF1 doesn't finish the race. It is won by the competition, who have well trained, highly experienced, drivers and pit crew. They win races and invest money back into new ideas and developments. They share a common vision of winning more and more Grand Prix and becoming the World Team Champions, again and again and again. They turn their car right into the winner's enclosure. The following week AMF1 closes down. They have run out of money. "Awful Management!"

Chapter 9 "Awful Management" Checklist

1. Have no sense of urgency – just relax.
2. Pack a case and leave.

"LEFT OR RIGHT?"

Chapter 10 – "Left or right?"

"Awful Management" has clear characteristics:

1. Management has insufficient knowledge or wisdom to run the organization successfully.
2. Management has no vision for the business, so employees are not motivated towards a common cause.
3. Management neither trains nor develops employees in support of the common cause.
4. Management has no inclination to listen to its employees or advisors.

Throughout "Awful Management" we have summarized each chapter with a checklist. Each element of these lists indicates yet another way to be seen as an awful Manager. I hope no readers want to be seen that way. I have read dozens of "Best Management Practice" books, and have the privilege of bringing up teenage sons. I know that most of us don't like being told what to do. We are free spirits. So the choice is yours – left for "Awful Management", or right for "Enlightened Management". The former is a short and easy journey. The latter is longer but leads to a happier team and better results.

"Awful Management" Checklists
Vision

1. Be unclear which products make money.
2. Have no clear vision for the business.
3. Avoid budgeting and 5-Year-Plans.

4. Do not share any hopes or dreams with the Team.
5. Particularly, do not engage or enthuse any Team Members.

Organization

1. Always be abusive to your employees.
2. Hold meetings without any agenda.
3. Ensure that the organization is unclear.
4. Do not allocate numerate objectives or responsibilities.
5 Never hold performance review meetings.
6. Do not develop or train the employees.
7 Ensure you have the best office. (You have earned it!)
8. Have no concern for employee working conditions.
9 Let the staff think you will run an appraisal process. (But don't.)

Unions

1. Always provide poor working conditions.
2. Pay no attention to health and safety.
3. Do not be fair in you approach to pay.
4. Do not be fair in your approach to people.
5. Do not be tempted to train or develop people.
6. Give no time whatsoever to union or employee representatives.
7. Only meet the above to inform them there are "no pay increases".
8. Embarrass employees in front of their mates.
9. Share no company information other than closures.
10. Ignore foreign culture and foreign language

Marketing

1. Ensure standard cost files are not up-to-date.
2. Better still, don't have any standard cost files.
3. Be unclear which products make you money.
4. Charge what you can, even at a loss.
5. Never go out into the market place – you might learn something
6. Promotion should be low key, but exhibitions are vital – socially.

Sales

1. It's relationships that matter - not higher prices and more business.
2. Only employ people who have comedy skills in sales.
3. Never train sales people - they may become a threat.
4. Let sales staff vent their feelings on the internet.

Cost Management

1. Always employee friends and family - ahead of talent.
2. Don't define where employees fit into the organization.
3. Never let employees know what you require of them.
4. Match car parking spots with employee numbers.
5. Eliminate HR procedures, so that you can sack at will.
6. Ignore all subsequent solicitor correspondence.
7. Only buy from long established friends.
8. Never challenge any price or invoice – you might offend.

9. Leave lights and heating running on a night, to dissuade burglars

10. Never change auditors or banks. New people might be nosier.

Quality

1. Have no specifications agreed with customers - keep it loose.

2. Have no Quality Procedures – keep it vague.

3. Have no time and respect for the Quality Department – a given.

4. Do not prioritize development projects.

5. Do not tightly project manage development projects.

6. Do not allow customers to trial new products before release.

7. Always source supplies from your friends – accept anything.

8. Have a "Do what the Hell you like culture" - control is creepy.

Look after the cash

1. Always spend more than you earn.

2. Let the Team decide how much to spend and on what.

3. Do no cash flow forecasting – these are just depressing guesses.

4. Ensure the warehouse is always full of stuff.

5. Pay suppliers quickly. They are your friends.

6. Don't chase customers for payment. They are your friends.

7. Invest in shiny equipment.

8. Invest in vague creative product development.

9. Keep bad news to yourself.
10. Hide excesses in containers at the back of the building.
11. Absolutely resist the appointment of a Turnaround Manager. They could be the death of you!

A sense of urgency
1. Have no sense of urgency – just relax.
2. Pack a case and leave.

Conclusion

"Enlightened Management" has clear characteristics:

1. Management has sufficient knowledge and wisdom to run the organization successfully.
2. Management has a vision for the business and use this to motivate employees towards a common cause.
3. Management trains and develops employees to their full potential, in support of the common cause.
4. Management listens to its employees and advisors.

Turn right please. Have fun. Thank you!

Gary